THE LIFE HISTORY
IN ANTHROPOLOGICAL
SCIENCE

L. L. LANGNESS
University of Washington

HOLT, RINEHART AND WINSTON

New York   Chicago   San Francisco   Toronto   London

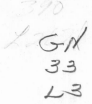

FOREWORD

About the Series

Anthropology has been, since the turn of the century, a significant influence shaping Western thought. It has brought into proper perspective the position of our culture as one of many, and has challenged universalistic and absolutistic assumptions and beliefs about the proper condition of man. Anthropology, the study of man, has been able to make this contribution mainly through its descriptive analyses of unfamiliar ways of life. Only in the last decades of anthropology's comparatively short existence as a science have anthropologists developed systematic theories about human behavior in its transcultural dimensions. Only still more recently have anthropological techniques of data collection and analysis become explicit.

Nearly every issue of every professional anthropological journal contains statements of methodological innovations. Our discipline is in a seminal period of development.

Teachers of anthropology have previously been handicapped by the lack of clear, authoritative statements of how anthropologists collect and analyze relevant data. The results of fieldwork are available in the ethnographers' published works. Although these demonstrate cultural diversity and integration, social control, religious behavior, marriage customs, and the like, they rarely tell students much about how the facts have been gathered and interpreted. Without this information the alert "consumer" of anthropological results is left uninformed about the processes of our science—an unsatisfying state of affairs for both the student and the professor.

Our Studies in Anthropological Method series is designed to help fill this gap. Each study in the series focuses upon some manageable aspect of modern anthropological methodology. Each one demonstrates significant aspects of the processes of gathering, ordering, and interpreting data. Some are highly selected dimensions of methodology. Others are concerned with the whole range of experience involved in studying a total society. The studies are written by professional anthropologists who have done fieldwork and have made significant contributions to the science of man and his works. The authors explain how they go about this work, and to what end. We believe the studies will be helpful to students—in courses ranging from the introductory to the graduate level—who want to know what processes of inquiry and ordering stand behind the formal, published results of anthropology.

About the Author

Lewis L. Langness is currently assistant professor of psychiatry and anthropology in the Department of Psychiatry, University of Washington School of Medicine. He has a B.S. degree in psychology from the University of Idaho where he also did graduate work in psychology. He holds an M.A. and Ph.D. in anthropology from the University of Washington. He has done fieldwork with the Clallam Indians of the Northwest Coast and more extensive work in New Guinea with the Bena Bena peoples of the eastern highlands. He has in preparation, with K. E. Read, *Peoples of Eastern New Guinea* and is also working on a biographical study of a New Guinea woman.

About the Book

This is the only integrative and systematic publication on the use of the life history in anthropology since Clyde Kluckhohn's well-known *The Personal Document in Anthropological Science,* published in 1945 by the Social Science Research Council. This is paradoxical, for as Dr. Langness points out, in one sense much of what any cultural anthropologist collects in the field and on which he bases his professional monographs is biographical in character.

In this study the author provides us with a most useful resource for understanding the place of biographical materials in anthropological research. First he reviews the relevant literature, starting far back in the nineteenth century and taking us up to the present. This gives the reader a systematic conception of the antecedents and present status of the biographical approach. He then discusses the theoretical context that gives life histories and other biographical materials their significance. The last half of the book is devoted to actual procedures involved in taking life histories in the field and some of the problems that are encountered in taking them. He also provides an exhaustive bibliography of biographical and methodological works, divided by the major periods corresponding to his review in Chapter 1.

We believe that this book will be extraordinarily useful to students in courses concerned mainly or in part with personality and culture, the individual in society, or psychological anthropology. It brings together insights and information about a very significant aspect of anthropological research and thinking in a clear and succinct manner.

GEORGE AND LOUISE SPINDLER
General Editors
Stanford, August 1965

PREFACE

The research in New Guinea, which forms a portion of this book, was conducted during the period January 1, 1961, to May 15, 1962. It was supported by a predoctoral fellowship and supplemental research grant from the National Institute of Mental Health, United States Public Health Service #M–4377. I wish to thank Karen Pataki and Lawrence Hennigh for their help in the collection of biographical materials.

L. L. LANGNESS

Seattle, Washington
August 1965

CONTENTS

THE LIFE HISTORY
IN ANTHROPOLOGICAL SCIENCE

Introduction

ANTHROPOLOGY is at once both a humanistic and a scientific enterprise. The range of anthropological interest is unsurpassed by any other discipline. Because of its broad scope and manifold subject matter the methodology of anthropology includes not only the more standard anthropological techniques such as participant-observation, the genealogical method, and controlled observations of behavior but also many techniques taken over from other disciplines. One finds anthropologists using such techniques as questionnaires, psychological tests, statistical analyses, and clinical interviewing along with dendrochronology, carbon-14 dating, stratigraphy, and glottochronology.

The biographical, or life history method, can by no means be considered unique to anthropology. It has, however, a distinctive history of development and use in this discipline. There are also certain problems involved in anthropological research using life histories which are not found in other settings, and, as I hope to show, the life history enjoys at the same time certain advantages over less intensive methods which commend it as an anthropological tool. Furthermore, in this age of interdisciplinary and behavioral science research, there is reason to believe that the biographical approach to human behavior offers a valuable common denominator for scholars in many disciplines—one that shows increasing signs of neglect.

It is not possible to deal with the use of life history materials without also considering in some way the general nature of anthropological fieldwork, problems of language and rapport, other methods and techniques, and the past, present, and probable future interests of anthropologists. Needless to say, this cannot all be done in one brief publication. It is difficult, indeed, to communicate the "process" of anthropological fieldwork, the "flavor" of another way of life, or the intensity and meaningfulness of the fieldwork situation for the individual researcher. One can hope only to communicate in some small way part of his own experience, some of the specific problems encountered and some of the hints which begin to emerge. As my own fieldwork experience has been in New

1

Guinea with the Bena Bena peoples of the eastern highlands, and to a lesser extent with the Clallam of the northwest coast of America, the brief examples offered are mostly from these areas.

Chapter 1 surveys the uses of biography from early in the nineteenth century to the present. Chapter 2 provides the necessary context of theory for the use of life histories. Chapters 3 and 4 discuss procedures for taking life histories and some of the problems encountered in their collection. An exhaustive bibliography of biographical studies in anthropology is provided as a resource for further study by the student.

1

The Uses of Life History to the Present

NTHROPOLOGICAL DATA are acquired almost exclusively through field-work. Anthropological fieldwork is conducted by the repeated perfor-mance of five fundamental tasks: watching, asking, listening, some-times *doing,* and recording. This would seem simple enough but is, in practice, exceedingly difficult and fraught with possibilities for error. The data accumu-lated can range from the most simple observation of the most simple artifact to a complex description of a complete religious system, none of which has actually been observed by the recorder. It is probably safe to say that the more the data are based upon direct observation the more accurate they are, the more they are based upon what one has been told the less accurate they are. The problems in-volved stem mostly from the personal biases of both observer and observed. It is this fact which has led in the past to the rejection of introspective accounts and to the development of extreme forms of behaviorism. The science of man de-mands, however, that all human behavior, introspective as well as any other, be taken into account. For the anthropologist to simply record controlled observa-tions of behavior in the absence of verbal accounts and introspection, although it might prove very amusing, would be absurd.

The anthropological fieldworker would like to have actually witnessed and had explained to him every significant event that occurs in the particular cul-ture he selected for study. For practical reasons such an ideal is never attained. It is entirely possible, for instance, that during, say, a year in the field, no one would die and hence no funeral would be witnessed. It is even more possible that in societies with elaborate initiation ceremonies for their young, no initiation would be held, or no one would get married, and so on. What the fieldworker takes home after his stint in the field is a record of all the events he has seen, plus descriptions and explanations of them by informants, plus a great many more descriptions of things he has not seen. It is always the case that he has in-

3

formation about many more things than he has actually witnessed. Because the researcher can only know these things through the words of his informants or through his own eyes and because each informant understands them only as they relate to his own unique history, and because the ethnologist can comprehend and record them only through his own idiosyncratic experience, we can say that, in this extreme sense, the bulk of the data are biographical. It is not completely far-fetched to assert that virtually all anthropology is biography. From this point of view, information elicited through psychological testing is simply a kind of stimulated, guided, and limited biography, as is the information gathered through the use of that oldest of anthropological devices, the genealogical method (Rivers 1900). But it is not biography in this very broad sense with which we are to be concerned in this book.

Biography, as the history of the life of an individual person, is used universally in the humanities, psychological, social and medical sciences, albeit for widely different purposes and with varying degrees of success. In history, for example, especially for those historians who subscribe to some variant of the "great man" type of history, biography can be the vehicle through which an entire era is protrayed. William L. Shirer's *The Rise and Fall of the Third Reich* (1959), fundamentally a biography of Adolf Hitler, is a good case in point.[1] In literature, biography often forms the core of short stories and novels, to say nothing of the art of biographical writing itself. One need think only of the short stories of Anton Chekhov, Thomas Wolfe's "A Portrait of Bascom Hawke" (1961), or the many examples of truly fine biographical and autobiographical writing.[2] The case study method of psychology and psychiatry, epitomized, for example, in Freud's "Analysis of a Phobia in a Five-Year-Old Boy" (1925) is well known. In medicine, in general, the first step is always to elicit biographical information (Blumer 1949). Biographical techniques have long been used in sociology, particularly since the impact of Thomas and Znaniecki's *The Polish Peasant in Europe and America* in 1918 (Dollard 1935; Angell 1945).

Biography, as the term is typically used, can mean either autobiography (a first person document) or biography per se (a third person document). Biography also appears under the labels, *personal document* or *human document*. Autobiographies are usually written records of a life by the subject himself. There are exceptions as, for example, *The Autobiography of Alice B. Toklas* written by Gertrude Stein (1933) or, more commonly, accounts written by anthropologists about nonliterate people on the basis of verbal materials provided by the subject. Because of the problems of interpretation, chronology, editing, and so on, which are involved in the gathering of biographical data in nonliterate cultures, and because of the difficulties involved in distinguishing biography from autobiography under these circumstances, it has been traditional in anthropology to use the term *life history* (Kluckhohn 1945; Aberle 1951). *Life history* will be used in this book to refer to an extensive record of a person's life as it is reported either by

---

[1] For material on the use of biography by historians see Gottschalk, 1945, and Mullett, 1963.

[2] Biography in literature has been well covered by Clifford, 1962, and Edel, 1959.

the person himself or by others or both, and whether it is written or in interviews or both.[3] The questions I will pursue here are: (1) How does one acquire a life history? (2) What does it mean? (3) What good is it? First, however, we should look at the history of the biographical approach to anthropological field work.

The Uses of Biography to 1925[4]

For reasons of convenience, as well as for other reasons which will become apparent, we can divide the development of the use of life history materials by anthropologists into three distinct periods: Up to 1925; from 1925 to 1944; from 1945 to the present.

During the nineteenth century in America, the frontiers were rapidly vanishing and the last of the great Indian wars were ending. There was great popular interest in the lives and personalities of certain American Indians, particularly those who received publicity or notoriety of any kind. This interest was, of course, of a romantic or sentimental kind and manifested itself mostly in written accounts of the "noble savage," the "vanishing red man," and similar tales. Naturally enough, Indian chiefs or famous warriors were the most popular subject matter. As early as 1832, B. B. Thatcher published *Indian Biography: or, An Historical Account of Those Individuals Who Have Been Distinguished among the North-American Natives as Orators, Warriors, Statesmen and Other Remarkable Characters.* Also during this early period, and later as well, many artists and travelers supplemented sketches or paintings with brief biographical remarks about their subjects. J. M. Stanley (1852) is the best example of this.

Somewhat later Dodd, Mead and Company began publishing a series called *Famous American Indians* (Eggleston and Seelye 1878), and in 1891 there appeared a "Who's Who" of "leading men of the Indian territory" (O'Beirne), and a life of Sitting Bull (Johnson). There were also at this time several full-length biographical accounts of such famous Indians at Black Hawk of the Sauk (Drake 1854), Pontiac of the Ottawa (Ellis 1861), Brant of the Mohawk (Anonymous 1872; Stone 1865), and two books of many many more to follow on Chief Joseph of the Nez Perce (Howard 1881; Lowe 1881). There were also full-length works on Uncas of the Mohicans (Stone 1842) and Se-Quo-Ya, who innovated the Cherokee alphabet (Foster 1885). This list is by no means exhaustive but merely names some of the most important documents of this early period. Samuel Drake's *The Aboriginal Races of North America* (1880) ran to at least 15 editions, and the three volumes by McKenny and Hall first appearing in 1836 came out in a new edition at late as 1933.

Probably the earliest known biographical work on a North American In-

---

[3] This definition departs importantly from that given by David Aberle (1951:1). I can see no reason for restricting the term to only first person accounts.

[4] This section draws heavily upon Kluckhohn's definitive survey (1945) and it cannot properly be referenced. I express my blanket appreciation of his pioneer effort.

dian was an autobiography published in 1825 (Anderson). Indeed, there were four other autobiographies before 1850. (Apes 1831; Black Hawk 1834; Cuffe 1939; and Copway 1847). All of these, including the first one, which was by a Christianized Cherokee, were heavily influenced by missionary propaganda with one exception. This is a book by a Sauk war leader and constitutes a plea for an end to white aggression toward the Indian and an attempt to justify his own conduct in warfare. Needless to say, all four of these autobiographies were the product of highly acculturated individuals. They also bear evidence of much white supervision and editing.

Prior to 1925 no real interest in biography as a specific tool for research had been shown by anthropologists and, as the major interest in writing biography was either literary, motivated by curiosity, or some personal motive, these are nonprofessional documents and we cannot be surprised that they contain little of either anthropological or psychological value. It is equally the case that what potential they have has never been exploited, a fact attributed by Clyde Kluckhohn to the notorious failure of anthropologists to do library research (1945:83). As the public interest in these popular accounts of Indians remains keen and has persisted to the present day, I shall say a little more about nonprofessional documents and then dismiss them as there is not the space to deal with them in any further detail.[5]

In 1900 an account appeared of an Indian divine (Love) and in 1906 *Lives of Famous Indian Chiefs* (Wood) and *Geronimo's Story of His Life* (Barrett) were published. In 1916, *The Princess Pocahontas* (Watson) appeared and was followed in the next year by *Ka-Mi-Akin, Last Hero of the Yakimas* (Splawn). In 1931 and 1938 there were popular accounts of still other chiefs (Chapin 1931; Britt 1938). Unusually well-documented biographies came out at about this time on Sequoya (Foreman 1938), Sacajawea (Hebard 1933), and Pocahontas (Garnett 1933). Frank Linderman wrote two very popular, somewhat sentimental accounts (1930, 1932) and Stanley Vestal wrote two sterling accounts of Sioux chiefs (1932, 1934). There appeared at about this time four volumes of personal reminiscences by three different Sioux Indians themselves (Eastman 1902; Neihardt 1932; Standing Bear 1928; 1933). In 1935 and 1936 biographies were published on Chief Joseph (Howard and McGrath 1935; Fee 1936). In 1938 *Tecumseh and His Times* (Oskison) appeared. Yellow Wolf, a Nez Perce, told his story for publication during this period. (McWhorter 1940). In 1941 Zimmerman published on White Eagle, a Ponca chief, and in 1943 a biography of Chief Seattle (Anderson 1943) was published. Since 1945 such books have appeared as *Red Men Calling on the Great White Father* (Turner 1951), an account of famous Indians who visited Washington, D.C. and called on the White House; *Chief Joseph of the Nez Perce* (Garst 1953); *Joseph Brant: Mohawk* (Chalmers and Monture 1955); and still another popular volume on Tecumseh (Tucker 1956). In 1962 a new book on Yellow Wolf was

---

[5] The division of biographies into "nonprofessional" and "professional" is an exceedingly arbitrary one. There are some biographies which technically are "nonprofessional" but which, because of their superior quality when judged by anthropological or psychological standards, will be treated as professional.

published (Chalmers). In 1963 a new and excellent popular historical biography of Chief Joseph and the Nez Perce War appeared (Beal). These titles serve only to indicate the unbroken interest in the lives of American Indians from the earliest American historical times right down to the present. This says nothing of the many informative reminiscences of white pioneers, the virtually uncountable children's books that have been published over the same long period of time as well as the thousands of articles and newspaper accounts. The unprecedented success of Theodora Kroeber's fine work, *Ishi in Two Worlds* (1961), for a book of its kind, indicates perhaps more than any other criterion the high degree of popular interest that remains today in the American Indian.

1925 to 1944

The publication, in 1926, of Paul Radin's famous *Crashing Thunder* most conveniently marks the beginning of truly rigorous work in the field of biography by professional anthropologists.[6] There had been, of course, some work of a "professional" nature much earlier. Among the earliest we find the well-informed observations of George Grinnell who lived and worked with the Pawnee (1889), Blackfoot (1892) and Cheyenne (1926); in *The Handbook of American Indians North of Mexico* (Hodge 1907) there are several brief biographical sketches. According to Kluckhohn, the first personal accounts published specifically as such by a professional anthropologist were three war narratives brought out by A. L. Kroeber in 1908 (Kluckhohn 1945:86). In 1919 Wallis used personal narratives in his account of the Sun Dance and in 1921 Edward Sapir published a short life of a Nootka Indian. Sapir's work, if not that of the others, reflects a growing interest in the individual at this time. This same interest can be seen in Germany where Schmidt, as early as 1906, made a plea for more studies of the individual. Koppers in 1924 published personal sketches of Tierra del Fuegians in a popular account of his fieldwork and another paper on an individual in the *Schmidt-Festschrift* in 1928. R. H. Lowie had a biographical account in the same volume. A somewhat different goal was pursued by Gilbert Wilson, who presented at about this same period some documents which, according to Kluckhohn, "are among the most distinguished and the most neglected products of American ethnology" (1945:88). Wilson attempted to present what nowadays would be called the *ethos* of Hidatsa culture, that is, the philosophy or world view as seen through the eyes of his informants themselves (1917, 1924, 1928). Truman Michelson also contributed importantly to the growing interest in biography at this time. Michelson wrote "autobiographies" of three native women, one a Fox (1925), one a Cheyenne (1932) and one an Arapaho (1933). These are of importance primarily because they were early attempts to present the female side of what remains even to this day a discipline very heavily male-oriented.

---

[6] Gordon Allport marks the publication of *The Polish Peasant* in 1920 as the turning point in the critical use of life history documents in sociology and phychology (1942:18).

Another trend was apparent at this time which is similar but probably not identical to that discussed above: the attempt to "humanize" anthropological materials. This influence can be seen in *American Indian Life,* a volume edited by Elsie Clews Parsons in 1922. This was a collection of essays for the lay public written by people working in anthropology. It included the biographical sketch published the year before by Sapir, several shorter biographical sketches, and a variety of other materials. Parsons had also published a biographical sketch in the preceding year. More or less the same kind of approach can be seen in Barbeau (1928), Harrington (1933), and Hilda Thurnwald (1937).

In historical perspective, unquestionably the greatest and most enduring influences on the sophisticated use of life history material were made by Edward Sapir and Paul Radin. Sapir's most significant contribution was the bridging of disciplines. Employing aspects of psychology and psychiatry as well as anthropological techniques, he greatly affected what is now called the culture-and-personality school. His influence can be seen in the work of Ruth Benedict, Ernest Beaglehole, and Walter Dyk, and consequently in the use of biography by anthropologists today. There also can be little doubt that Sapir was himself influenced by Harry Stack Sullivan and that Sapir's interest in life history materials thus paralleled his interest is psychology and psychiatry. Radin's interest in life history materials seems to have been motivated by very different kinds of reasons, but they had an equal if not greater impact on subsequent work in biography.

Radin published, as early as 1913, a brief autobiography of a Winnebago Indian. In 1920 he published a longer one in which he argued that biographical information was needed to supplement the more usual anthropological accounts:

> . . . the aim being, not to obtain autobiographical details about some definite personage, but to have some representative middle-aged individual of moderate ability describe his life in relation to the social group in which he had grown up . . . (1920:384).

It is clear that Radin, unlike Sapir, was interested only in *culture* and not in the individual per se, the "individual-in-culture," or in personality. Radin's interest in biography as a cultural rather than psychological or psychocultural document, as opposed to Sapir's, tended to remain the dominant although not the exclusive one until approximately 1945. Radin revised, added to, and republished his 1920 work which became *Crashing Thunder.* This was a work of great influence and stimulated many other anthropologists to use biographical data. It was not, however, by design or intent psychologically oriented, and it was not truly in the culture-and-personality tradition which was developing in parallel. To understand this, it is necessary to look at the anthropology of the 1920s in retrospect.

American anthropology during the early part of this century was, generally speaking, nontheoretical and anti-evolutionary. Franz Boas, virtually single-handedly trained or influenced a generation of scholars who were, with some exceptions, more concerned with collecting and recording ethnographic facts than with analyzing them. The impact of Radcliffe-Brown and Malinowski was not yet apparent, nor was the influence of Sapir significant at this time. There was the feeling that as American Indian cultures were fast disappearing it was critical to salvage as much as possible. Analyses could come later. Many scholars were engaged on the reservations and elsewhere in this type of recording and in many cases there were few available informants who were able to tell the ethnographer in any articulate, integrated manner just what the traditional way of life had been like. Given this atmosphere, it is not surprising that Radin looked for a "representative middle-aged individual" and, later, a "primitive philosopher" (1927).

In any event, it does seem to be the case that the bulk of the specifically anthropological biography between 1925 and 1945 was directed towards clarifying or portraying the cultural dimension of human existence rather than the idiosyncratic or psychological dimension.[7] Furthermore, it was methodologically unsound in that only rarely did the authors specify how the materials were elicited, what the relationship between observer and observed has been, how much editing had been done, or what rearranging was involved. Often the materials were badly organized. In some cases there were no ethnographic annotations. In other cases the annotations were incomplete or inadequate. This was not true of all works published during this time, however, and there were some worthwhile exceptions among both professional and nonprofessional documents. Some nonprofessional works of exceptional merit during this time were Ntara's *Men of Africa* (1934), Gollock's *Lives of Eminent Africans* (1928), *Ten Africans* (Perham 1936), Sach's *Black Hamlet* (1937), the story of Turi, the Lapp (Hatt (1931) and Heluiz Washburne's "autobiography" of an Eskimo woman (1940).

Among the finest of the professional documents during this time are: Dyk's *Son of Old Man Hat* (1938); Underhill's "autobiography" of a Papago woman (1936); the exceptional work of Gorer on the Lepchas (1938); Ford's *Smoke from Their Fires* (1941); Radin's *Crashing Thunder*, of course; and Leo Simmons' *Sun Chief* (1942). Both Landes (1938) and Morris Opler (1938, 1939, 1941) made use of biographical materials at this time as did Redfield and Villa (1934), Julian Steward (1934, 1938), and Leslie White 1943). F. E. Williams recorded the reminiscences of Ahuia Ova (1939) and Gladys Reichard wrote a slightly fictionalized biographical account of a Navaho woman (1939) which had been preceded by a similar attempt in 1934.

There was clearly an upsurge in interest in the use of biography and the published biographies tended to become much better from a professional point of view toward the end of the period. The improvement was probably due to the fact that beginning in about 1935 serious attention was focused for the first time on the methodological problems involved in the use of life histories and related matters. In sociology, John Dollard's *Criteria for the Life History* (1935) served as the stimulus for an heightened interest in methodology. This affected the fields of sociology, anthropology, and psychology alike for a time but, as we shall see, the interest crested approximately ten years later and then diminished somewhat. It is most interesting to note that Dollard's work reflects, again, the over-all interest of the period in using life histories to reflect cultural facts, for

---

[7] See Kluckhohn (1945:88–91) for specific comments on the most important works during this period.

Dollard devoted himself almost exclusively to showing the importance of the culture concept and how biographical materials must be seen in a cultural rather than purely psychological dimension. Gordon Allport later criticized Dollard's work on the grounds of this "cultural bias" (1942), but this in no way detracts from the great interest stimulated by Dollard's insightful work.

In addition to book reviews of biographical and autobiographical documents, which naturally were concerned with methodological considerations, there appeared during this period many articles in anthropology, sociology and psychology dealing with the more specific problems of taking life histories and fieldwork. Paul Radin brought out a volume on methodology in 1933. Margaret Mead suggested more comprehensive field methods in 1933 and in 1939 wrote on the problems involved in the use of native languages as fieldwork tools. This prompted almost immediate replies from Elkin (1941), Lowie (1940) and Jules Henry (1940). Lowie in his fine work on the Crow (1935), had commented earlier on the problems of using American Indian languages. In 1937 Reckless and Selling compared psychiatric and sociological interviewing and Cora DuBois wrote on psychological objectives and techniques in ethnography. Schapera wrote on field methods for studying culture contact (1935). S. F. Nadel wrote a brief article on problems of interviewing (1939) and Richards did an essay in the same year on the development of fieldwork methods. Blumer prepared an extensive critique of *The Polish Peasant* at the request of the Social Science Research Council in 1939 and in the same year Cartwright and French questioned the reliability of life history materials. Then in 1940 an article on the participant-observer technique by Florence Kluckholn appeared and in 1942 Herbert Passin wrote a perceptive article on prevarication as a problem in fieldwork. In 1945 the Social Science Research Council sponsored new work on the use of personal documents, which still remains the definitive account for anthropologists (Kluckhohn). It is well worth our effort to consider Kluckhohn's (1945:102–103) summary of life history data and generalizations up to 1945:

1. A considerable number of popular and historical biographical and autobiographical documents, of widely varying quality, exist. These have not as yet been systematically exploited by anthropologists.

2. The number of professional studies is steadily growing. However, the following limitations upon the adequacy of existent materials must be recognized:

a) The vast majority are too sketchy and too limited to objective events. They do not give even the shadow of a life—merely the partially outlined skeleton.

b) The different age and sex groups are very unevenly represented. Almost all of the subjects were fifty years of age or over at the time of giving their autobiography, and the vast majority are men.

c) With the exception of about half a dozen tribes, there is no basis for comparison of life histories within the same culture and hence of judging whether or not a particular document is a representative sample.

d) Annotation is very meager and almost exclusively of an ethnographic character. Analysis and interpretation have only begun to appear.

e) The conditions under which and the techniques by which data have been obtained are very inadequately specified.

f) Published biographical materials are, at best, only very generally and roughly comparable because conditions and techniques are either unknown or, where at least partially described, so very different.

There has been a shift in emphasis as well as increasing activity in the field of life histories since about 1944. The biographical materials now available are too extensive to be adequately reviewed here. We can consider changes in orientation and merely select a few representative examples to see how well they have succeeded or failed in overcoming the limitations set forth above.

1944 to the Present

In the years 1944–45, interest in culture-and-personality and hence the interest in the individual, which can be traced to Edward Sapir, and interest in the use of life history materials, which had been stimulated by Paul Radin, began to converge. The first evidence of the merger of these techniques are two very influential and related works, Cora DuBois' masterful *The People of Alor* (1944) and Abram Kardiner's *The Psychological Frontiers of Society* (1945). These two books are by no means the only ones at this time to express an interest in the individual or in culture-and-personality, but they do represent the most important conscious attempt to use life history materials in a cultural context for the purpose of getting at distinctive personality types. The thesis of primary and secondary institutions (that is, cultural variables) with personality as an intervening (that is, psychological) variable was a very important theoretical landmark, and the acceptance of this mode of thinking made the use of life history data a necessity. Although there is no need to dwell on this, it may be helpful to look at a brief excerpt from *The Psychological Frontiers of Society:*

> For the purpose of substantiating the thesis of this book one biography in a culture will hardly suffice. We must have an adequate sampling of sex, age, and status differentiations, and no arbitrary number can be regarded as adequate. We need a sufficient number to make adequate comparisons, but it is more important to find where the deviations are. As we progress in our study of biographies we note the banal fact that no two in the same culture are alike. But the deviants are as important to us as the norms.
>
> The uses of the biographies are numerous. Here is our first chance to see whether our guess about the kind of personality a given set of institutions will create is at all approximated in reality. We can reverse the procedure and operate from personalities to institutions. It is only in a biography that we can see how the various institutions are functionally articulated (Kardiner 1945:37).

Notice here that the interest in culture is not given up in favor of an interest in personality. Rather, an interest in personality is added to the earlier anthropological interest. Kardiner's book had a profound influence on subsequent anthropology. The culture-and-personality discipline is now firmly established and the reciprocal relations postulated by Kardiner remain in the forefront of interest. Unfortunately, the use of the life history does not.

In addition to the influence of Kardiner and DuBois and the emergence of culture-and-personality as an anthropological interest, there have been, since the 1920s, other developments which could have led to an increased interest in the use of life history data. These developments are: (1) the interest in studies of values (Bidney 1953), (2) the now well-established interest in culture change and acculturation (Beals 1953), and (3) the growth of the behavioral science movement, particularly as it relates to medicine (Caudill 1953). However, as Honigmann (1961:96) has recently pointed out for culture-and-personality research, there has not been a parallel interest in the use of life histories. Some idea of the neglect can be seen in *Psychological Anthropology* (Hsu 1961), which consists of fifteen articles, all either methodological or surveys of culture-and-personality research. Of the fifteen articles, only four, including Honigmann's, even mention the life history, and then only in the most incidental fashion. While it is true that for the period roughly from 1925 to 1944 there was increased interest in the use of biographical materials, it does not seem to have been sustained although the demand for such materials in the post-1945 period has probably been greater than ever before.

In order to understand this paradox, and before asking why it is so, let us look at some of the more recent uses of life histories. In this way we can also review the major uses of the life history approach.

The use of life history materials for the ultimate understanding of *culture* has remained fundamental and can be seen in somewhat different forms in the post-1945 literature. The aims of Gilbert Wilson, for example, and perhaps his direct influence as well, can be seen in a work by Alfred Bowers, *Mandan Social and Ceremonial Organization* (1950). This interesting study also reflects the pattern of earlier American anthropology in salvaging disappearing cultures as it is based upon extensive interviewing of only fourteen informants with the aim of learning what their culture meant to them:

> In recording the data contained in this report, I encouraged informants to express in their own way meanings which customs had for them; and this report is an attempt to describe Mandan culture in terms of its meaning to the Mandan Indians (1950:viii).

Bowers' study does not contain extensive life history materials per se but it is importantly based upon them and he has much unpublished biographical data. Unfortunately, both Wilson's and Bowers' work have been sadly neglected.

The use of personal documents as a foundation for describing culture appears to be much more common since the work of DuBois and Kardiner and others, but at the same time there seems not to have been the concentration upon the biographies themselves that might have been expected. When biographies per se do appear they tend to be used (1) to portray culture; (2) for literary purposes; (3) in connection with culture change (4) to portray some aspect of culture not usually portrayed by other means (such as the "women's view"): (5)

to answer some theoretical question in culture-and-personality; (6) to communicate something not usually communicated (for example, the humanistic side of anthropology) ; (7) in some combination of two or more of these objectives. These usages never appear in pure form and there is always some overlap.

In studies designed to portray a culture, a person is usually selected who is a most typical or representative member of a culture. Probably the best recent example of this type of work is *Juan the Chamula* by Ricardo Pozas (1962). This book, according to the author, "should be considered a small monograph on the culture of the Chamulas" (1962:1). In addition, the book attempts to give insights about the process of culture change, and it also has some literary merit. Like so many of the earlier studies of this kind, there is no explanation of precisely how the raw data were gathered, how extensive they were, how much editing was done, or what the relationship between author and subject was. There also appears to be little recognition of the limitations of just one life history for the purpose of portraying an entire culture and there is little analysis of any kind beyond a brief summary of what a typical Chamula is supposed to be like. A similar use of biographical materials, on a slightly smaller scale for for the same purpose, can be seen in an article by Robert Glasse (1959). He attempts to give an idea of certain details of Huli culture by using three male life histories selected as representative of three different status positions. This type of approach is highly commendable and does give a much better sampling of the culture.

Oscar Lewis is beyond question the greatest proponent of the life history. He has produced by far the most detailed, lucid, and, from a literary point of view, the most moving and aesthetic biographies to date. Lewis's *Five Families* (1959), although not a life history approach, represents a valuable innovation in ethnological research and led to *The Children of Sanchez* (1961), which does represent a purely biographical approach. *The Children of Sanchez,* widely recognized as a literary masterpiece, also represents a valuable cultural and psychological document and is probably the finest biographical account written by an anthropologist to date. This book does have important advantages over single life histories as Lewis himself observes:

> In my research in Mexico since 1943, I have attempted to develop a number of approaches to family studies. In *Five Families,* I tried to give the reader some glimpses of daily life in five ordinary Mexican families, on five perfectly ordinary days. In this volume I offer the reader a deeper look into the lives of one of these families by the use of a new technique whereby each member of the family tells his own life story in his own words. This approach gives us a cumulative, multifaceted, panoramic view of each individual, of the family as a whole, and of many aspects of lower-class Mexican life. The independent versions of the same incidents given by the various family members provide a built-in check upon the reliability and validity of much of the data and thereby partially offset the subjectivity inherent in a single autobiography. At the same time it reveals the discrepancies in the way events are recalled by each member of the family.

This method of multiple autobiographies also tends to reduce the element of investigator bias because the accounts are not put through the sieve of a middle-class North American mind but are given in the words of the subjects themselves. In this way, I believe I have avoided the two most common hazards in the study of the poor, namely, oversentimentalization and brutalization. Finally, I hope that this method preserves for the reader the emotional satisfaction and understanding which the anthropologist experiences in working directly with his subjects but which is only rarely conveyed in the formal jargon of anthropological monographs (1961:xi).

Expressed here is Lewis's interest in the culture of poverty (the traditional anthropological interest in studying *culture* through life histories) and in communicating some of the more humanistic aspects of anthropological research. Lewis also gives some account of his relationship to his subjects and how he acquired the raw data. Virtually the only criticism one can make of Lewis's work is that it is almost exclusively descriptive and involves very little in the way of analysis or "problem-orientation." This is not a fair criticism is so far as one can only criticize a work with respect to how well the author fulfills his aims and Lewis's aims are primarily descriptive. In *Children of Sanchez* one finds, then, a masterful descriptive account of urban poverty as seen through the eyes of the family members. One also acquires many insights into the personalities of the family members and the effects of the culture of poverty on personality formation. There is little concern with theoretical relationships between personality and social structure, between the motives of the actors and their choice of alternative actions, or with the effects of such personalities upon the culture itself. In *Pedro Martinez* (1964), which is similar in design to *The Children of Sanchez,* but which deals with a rural family rather than an urban one, Lewis makes more of an attempt to suggest such relationships. In this way if no other *Pedro Martinez* is the stronger of the two works from the strictly anthropological point of view. Taking into account every aspect of these works by Lewis, it becomes apparent that they are more humanistic and literary than they are scientific.

Worker in the Cane, a Puerto Rican life history by Sidney Mintz (1960), is somewhat similar to the work of Oscar Lewis in that it deals with poverty, with a lower-class individual, and is based upon more than one person's account. Although it does not possess quite the same literary merit, it gives a much better view of the author's role in the acquisition of the material and makes considerably more use of analysis. Mintz makes no pretensions about how representative the case is and presents his material mainly on the basis of its intrinsic human interest.

Life histories are often used to portray some aspect of either culture or anthropology or both that otherwise is believed to have been neglected. It is primarily for this reason that life histories of women have increased in number during the past twenty years. One interesting but non-ethnographic attempt to present a woman's view is *Zula Woman* by Rebecca Reyher (1948), who posed somewhat dramatically the following questions:

What did Zulu women do? How did they manage lifelong marriage? Were they happy? Was polygamy, as my sophisticated friends assured me, a natural state of man? Was it possible to love with one's body freely and easily, capturing the spirit and taming it to its primary needs? Didn't Zulu women get notions, too? Were the heart and soul of a primitive women different from mine, or those of the women I knew? (1948:xii.)

A similar but much more adequate account of selected aspects of a woman's life also published in 1948 was Alice Marriott's *Maria: The Potter of San Ildefonso*. An exceedingly good full-length autobiography of a Hausa woman by M. F. Smith appeared in 1954. In addition to giving a woman's perspective it:

. . . is valuable from two different points of view: as a record of Hausa life it is unique in the detail, the time-span, the variety of aspects and events, and above all in its immediacy; but it is significant also to the social anthropologist with structural interests as a documentation of the extent to which, and the precise way in which, structure governs and shapes an individual life. A great deal has recently been written on a variety of postulated relationships between "culture" and "personality"; this record will have served a useful function if it suggests ways in which the individual's life-process and its relations to the social structure can be studied in greater detail with a diachronic perspective (M. G. Smith, 1954:14).

In 1961, Nancy Lurie published a shorter but equally good autobiographical account, *Mountain Wolf Woman*. It is especially valuable in that the subject was the sister of Radin's subject, Crashing Thunder. In 1962, Louise Spindler did a valuable study of culture change using female life histories. This, again, has exceptional merit because it complements the previous work done by George Spindler on the same subject using only male informants. Denise Paulme edited at about this time the volume *Women of Tropical Africa* (1963), which is a collection of six essays, dealing specifically with the position of women in African societies. Most of them are based in some measure on biographical data, the one by Laurentin actually includes biographical sketches. A recent study of great sensitivity as well as of ethnographic value is *Black Background: The Childhood of a South African Girl* (Blacking 1964). The author combines his own ethnographic knowledge of Venda culture with the short written sketches of a seventeen-year-old native girl and the result is a very pleasing if "tiny slice of their fascinating culture" (1964:10).

There are certain aspects of culture that the anthropologist wishes to record that necessitate a biographical approach virtually by definition. Dreams are a good example of this as are hallucinations, trances, religious experiences, and other similar things. Unfortunately, we cannot go into these phenomena here. There is, however, another use of biography which we need to consider and that has to do with the "humanistic" nature of anthropological science. I have already mentioned the first work of this kind edited by Elsie Clews Parsons. Probably the best example of this recently is the fine book edited by Joseph B. Casagrande, *In the Company of Man* (1960). The aim of books like this is not only to give the reader some insight into another culture but also to communicate what the process of "doing anthropology" is like—that is, to transmit the "flavor" of fieldwork:

Field research is a challenging scientific undertaking, an adventure of both the mind and the spirit. It is also a memorable *human* experience, yet most anthropological writings tend to obscure the fact. Concerned with cultural patterns and norms, we are accustomed in articles and monographs to treat our data at a highly abstract level several stages removed from the vividness and immediacy of what we have experienced in the field. In our published work remarkably little is vouchsafed about personal reactions to the vicissitudes of field work and to the people among whom we have lived and worked. Most particularly, significant relationships with individuals who have been our close associates for many months are as a rule memorialized in a mere footnote or a few brief prefatory sentences (Casagrande 1960:xii).

This work, like many of the others I have discussed, has little theoretical significance. This is not meant as a criticism since the intent of these books was not theoretical but, generally speaking, either literary, descriptive, or humanistic. Deserving of discussion also are more "problem-oriented" uses of biographical data. In this category we find two types of materials: those dealing with culture change and those dealing with the theoretical questions inherent in the culture-and-personality approach.

Many of the studies which have been mentioned thus far, in addition to their primary objectives, have also been concerned with the phenomena of culture change. The concern has been with varying degrees of emphasis but has tended to be secondary to some other aim or at most only one interest among several. In some works culture change has been the key focus, and studies of culture change have been an obvious place for the use of life history materials. Although there has long been controversy over the relevance of psychology for anthropology, this has been less true of scholars interested specifically in culture change or acculturation. Indeed, one of the first articles to use the term "acculturation" (written by Richard Thurnwald in 1932) was entitled "The Psychology of Acculturation" (Beals 1953:624). The interest in psychology has been accompanied by an interest in the individual and his personality characteristics and, thus, in life history data. The widespread interest in psychology on the part of students of acculturation is probably explained by two related facts: (1) Virtually no aspect of culture change can be explained by the mere fact of culture contact alone. The simple fact of culture contact cannot itself explain nativistic movements, anomie, excessive drinking, and other bizarre or undesirable consequences of change which have been so widely reported. It has been necessary to postulate the presence of psychological variables such as feelings of inferiority, despair, envy, impotence, guilt, and so on, as well as to deal with such concepts as motivation, attitude, cognition, and stress, all researchable primarily through individual cases. (2) Related to this is the widespread belief that those individuals in the forefront of change are the deviants, the disgruntled, and the unhappy; those who have nothing to lose and are thus believed to be motivated to change. In either case the usefulness of the life history is manifest.

There are many studies of change that utilize extensive biographical materials. There was, for example, a very interesting study, "Personality Under Social Catastrophe," utilizing ninety life histories of the Nazi revolution (Allport,

Bruner, and Jandorf 1948). In a more intensive and more traditional manner, life histories were collected and used very successfully by such writers as Laura Thompson (1950) working with the Hopi, by Evon Vogt with the Navaho (1951), and by the Spindlers in their work on Menomini acculturation mentioned earlier. With respect to the theory of deviation just mentioned, there have been such efforts as H. G. Barnett's study of Indian Shakers (1957), which deals at some length with the life of John Slocum, founder of the movement. Barnett discusses some other deviant individuals, although not at great length, in *Being a Palauan* (1960). In this case Barnett uses the life histories for reasons I have not yet mentioned:

> Men like Daob inevitably come to the attention of a close observer of village life, for they are undoubtedly a significant part of it. They may affect it little or not at all, but their deviations and failures are significant for an appreciation of the conformance and successes of others. They are conspicuous because they throw into relief the salient features of the life around them, a spectacle in which they figure as observers rather than participants. Their role is not entirely passive; often they are outspoken skeptics and critics. Whatever their peculiarities may be, it is important to appreciate that there are deviant personalities in Palau, if for no other reason than to offset the prevalent opinion that "primitive" societies are homogeneous entities, solid blocks of colorless conformers. Some Palauans are no different from some Americans in that they do not like some of the most cherished customs of their associates (1960:65).

The title, "Marginal Men: A Study of Two Half-Caste Aborigines" (Beckett 1958), reflects a similar interest. M. G. Smith has written about a cult leader (1959) as has Schwartz (1962). Mandelbaum's title "A Reformer of His People," (1960) and Voget's "A Shoshone Innovator" (1950) again make the point. There is also Maher's fine book on culture change, *New Men of Papua* (1961), in which he discusses the life and influence of Tommy Kabu on Purari culture. For the even more psychologically inclined there is a fine collection, *Clinical Studies in Culture Conflict* by Georgene Seward (1958). Such contemporary biography as that of Jomo Kenyatta (Delf 1962), and the autobiographies of Luthuli (1962), and Chief Awolawo (1960) also deal importantly with culture change.

As Whiting and Child (1953) indicated, there are basically three kinds of culture-and-personality relationships to be considered: (1) the effects of culture on personality; (2) personality as an intervening variable between two cultural variables; (3) the effects of personality upon culture. There have been surprisingly few life history studies devoted more or less exclusively to analyzing in detail any of these theoretical relationships. This is all the more amazing when one considers the number of purely theoretical works which have appeared on the subject of culture-and-personality during the past twenty years. Furthermore, with the exception of "Gregorio, the Hand Trembler" (Leighton and Leighton 1949), the few studies that have been made have all been psychoanalytically oriented and have dealt strictly with culture contact and deviation (categories 1 and 2 mentioned before). That is, there have been no studies dealing with the effects of personality on culture, the closest to this being analyses of deviant individuals or, in history, studies of "great men."

David Aberle's "The Psychosocial Analysis of a Hopi Life History" is one of the best attempts to systematically analyze the effect of Hopi culture on an individual personality. Aberle also uses the life history to reconcile seemingly diverse views of Hopi culture (Aberle 1951a, 1951b), and it is one of the few studies not concerned with modal personality, following Kardiner. Even so, it also fails to deal adequately with the mutual two-way relationships specified by the culture-and-personality approach.

Gladwin and Sarason (1953, 1959), stimulated by Kardiner, attempted to demonstrate a *range* of personality types on Truk rather than simply one modal type, and Hart (1954) wrote an article criticizing what he believed to be Kardiner's oversimplification. Although Kardiner's work stimulated a great deal of further research, it does not appear to have stimulated the extensive use of the life history approach per se, nor do Kluckhohn's repeated urgings in this direction seem to have had much effect. Indeed, unfortunate as it seems, we can use virtually unchanged the summary statements made by Kluckhohn in 1945. The only attempt to approximate Kluckhohn's criteria for a life history is William Sayre's *Sammy Louis* (1956), which combines many of the scientific aims of the life history approach plus a related one we have not yet mentioned. The work portrays Micmac culture, and it is concerned with the effect of culture on personality, effects of culture change, and effect of culture on what one might consider a special aspect of personality, mental health.

With respect to the effects of culture on mental health, which necessarily involve case studies of individuals, there have been many articles in recent years. Seligman wrote on temperament and psychosis as early as 1929. Cooper wrote on the Wiitiko Psychosis in 1933. Morgan wrote on "human wolves" among the Navaho in 1936. A. I. Hallowell was a pioneer here as he has been in culture-and-personality in general (1934, 1938, 1939), and Beaglehole wrote on psychosis in Hawaii in 1939. Bingham Dai wrote on personality problems in Chinese culture in 1941, and Cannon wrote his well-known account of "voodoo death" in 1942. Molina wrote about a psychopathic personality in Guatemala in 1947. J. C. Carothers wrote on the subject of mental derangement in Africans in 1948 and in the same year Gillin wrote a famous article on "magical fright." Barnouw did an article on phantasy among the Chippewa in 1949, Jewell wrote an account of a psychotic Navajo in 1952, and similar studies have been made including those by Spindler (1952), Spiro (1950, 1959), Newman (1964), and Langness (1965). Studies of this kind, utilizing life history data, have done a great deal to demonstrate relationships between culture and mental illness and add credence to postulations of other relationships between culture-and-personality that have not been so easy to demonstrate. It appears, however, that aside from the kinds of studies in which life history materials are critical, there has been an emphasis in recent years on other means of obtaining data—mainly on psychological testing, observations of behavior coupled with brief statements by many informants, or restricted interviewing. While these are useful and important ways of obtaining

information, they should be rounded out with interviewing in depth and intensive life history taking of a more clinical variety, even though this is more difficult and time consuming.

Summary

In summary, we can see that there has long been an interest in life histories. In the pre-1925 era, this took the form of nonprofessional biographical and autobiographical studies of a sentimental, romantic kind which purported to show the "noble savage" at his best, or sometimes worst, and which had wide popular appeal. Largely due to the influence of Paul Radin and Edward Sapir, the first professional interest was shown in personal documents about 1925. Between 1925 and 1944 there was an increasing interest in the use of life history material and also an increasing interest in methodology and the problems of methodology. During this same period of time, the interest in culture-and-personality stimulated by Sapir, Ruth Benedict, Margaret Mead, and others was creating still further interest in the individual and in psychology. These two trends met in 1944–45 and, with the publication of Kardiner's *The Psychological Frontiers of Society,* new importance was attached to life histories; the anthropological interest was formally expanded to include personality as a significant unit for analysis. Neither Kardiner's use of life histories nor Kluckhohn's arguments for their use resulted in an extensive development of the life history, although some good studies were stimulated. The interest which peaked between 1925 and 1945 appears to have diminished somewhat and there has been an emphasis on less time consuming and less difficult methods of gathering data. The actual uses of the life history have been limited to the kinds of studies discussed.

2

Potential Uses of the Life History

K LUCKHOHN REMARKED, in his 1945 account of the use of life histories, that his most salient conclusion had to do with the deficiencies found in the analysis and interpretation of such documents (1945:133). With some rare but notable exceptions the same conclusion can be drawn today. Kluckhohn did set very high standards it is true, but even when measured against lesser ones the available published materials are sadly inadequate when it comes to interpretation and analysis. What one wishes to analyze is, of course, determined by his orientation and aims, that is, whether he is a student of change, social structure, material culture, personality, or what have you. In the case of existent life histories the lack of analysis and interpretation is ubiquitous. The life history can scarcely be said to have been exploited to its fullest in those cases mentioned in the preceding chapter, nor has it been exploited in the many other areas where it might have been.

In the preceding chapter I discussed the purposes for which the life history actually has been used. In this chapter I will examine these in more detail, mention some potential uses of the life history in areas in which they have not been so extensively used, and discuss some of the problems of analysis and interpretation. I will attempt to show that the contemporary problems of interest to anthropologists indicate a greater emphasis upon life history data than has hitherto been shown; that the shifts to psychological testing and other methods, although in keeping with the ever-present trend toward scientific objectivity, are not adequate for the kinds of data needed in most areas of current interest; and that if suggested reorientations in anthropology come about they will become even more inadequate.

Culture and Idiosyncracy

As we have seen, the bulk of the life history work to the present has continued to be descriptive and concerned with biography as a cultural document. As such, the most obvious requirement should be that it is an accurate description of the culture. For cultures previously unreported it would be desirable if we could accept the life history of one or just a few individuals as an accurate (though partial) description of the culture. This can be accomplished only if the biographer indicates the parts of the document that report culture patterns and what part reflects the idiosyncratic. Biographers have seldom bothered to make this clear. In cases where there are already ethnographic facts known, the biography should be exploited to the point of confirming old facts, offering new ones, or explaining the reasons for differences of opinion about ethnographic facts where such discrepancies occur.

Deviance

No culture is so rigid as completely to prohibit deviance from the accepted patterns. There is always a discrepancy between the cultural rules, or ideals, and the actual behavior exhibited. It is important to know what the accepted range of variation is, and the life history is a good method of investigating this aspect of a culture. That is, how deviant can individuals be? How free is an individual to pursue his own desires within the limits set by the culture?[1] It is equally important to know what the sanctions are against deviance, how severe they are, if they apply equally to all categories of person, and how they affect the person against whom they are used. Related to this is the problem of "covert" or "implicit" culture. In any culture, for the participants, there are a series of assumptions which are usually unstated but which are shared and tacitly understood by the actors and which importantly influence their behavior. This is part of the "inside" view of culture frequently mentioned in anthropology but exceedingly difficult to uncover and understand. The analysis of intensive, "clinical," life histories is the best method for attempting to deal with this although it seems seldom to have been attempted.

Cultural Structure

There is, in addition, the problem of cultural structure which is fundamentally a problem in cross-cultural epistemology. It is exceedingly difficult to be completely free of ethnocentrism as there is always the problem of categorizing and labeling different aspects of culture. Anthropological note taking and report-

---

[1] An interesting attempt to demonstrate individual actions as opposed to norms for behavior can be found in a recent work by Philip Newman (1965) in which he offers several individual accounts as examples of "cultural freedom."

ing usually divides enthnographic facts into economics, politics, religion, and similar categories although it is recognized that the culture in question does not so divide up the world. A biography, particularly one which was collected in a nondirective manner—the informant more or less freely associates—need not be contained within the limits of externally imposed categories; thus it is probably the best way to get insight into the cultural structure as perceived and felt by the people themselves. The classification of things and the interdependence between them, difficult for the anthropologist to understand because of his ethnocentric bias, can be best approached through the analysis of many individual accounts. Here again, the existing biographical studies have not been exploited.

Culture Change

The analysis and understanding of culture change, as indicated earlier, involves in a very crucial way certain psychological variables and thus should constitute an important area for the use of individual life histories. In this area of research, however, although there has been much emphasis on the individual innovator, the leader, the deviant, and so on, and, although there are some good biographical sketches of such individuals, the trend has been more toward psychological testing and supplemental information rather than toward intensive life history taking and analysis. This is all the more remarkable in view of the still very crude generalizations we have about the phenomena of change. Even though there are good grounds for believing that certain types of individuals are in the forefront of change, whether these be the disgruntled, the deviant, or the community leaders, there are few detailed analyses of individual cases. This is rather astounding because so many hypotheses of change are couched in psychological terms or implicitly contain them. A good example of this is from Keesing (1953:89):

> As an example of the type of hypothesis which has been set up for testing in the field, one which gives a very broad frame of reference might be compounded on the basis of leads in a number of recent works. Its propositional frame could run something like this. . . . So far as they feel superior, in relation to groups and individuals with whom they are in contact, their culture may be held to the more firmly, or change may go further with little tension. By contrast, to the extent that groups and individuals come to feel themselves inferior, lose confidence in their basic sources of security, power and prestige, and so lapse in morale, the way is opened for extensive and even drastic change.

This broad hypothesis (inferiority brings about change) arrived at "on the basis of leads in a number of recent works," defines a basic frame of reference widely held by scholars of change. It is worth examining in more detail because it points up some of the inadequacies in anthropological methodology which, in turn, make increasingly apparent the need for more intensive life history materials.

If one looks at the literature on culture change, it immediately becomes apparent that there are grave problems in establishing that superior-inferior feelings are involved at all. First, many works on culture change are purely historical. Such studies cannot be used as the basis for hypotheses specifying psychological states of mind. There is no way of discerning the kinds of psychological states of mind that prevailed. Second, a large number of anthropological studies of culture change are based upon data obtained through the standard anthropological procedures of observation and interviews with a great variety of informants. The anthropologists gathering the information were not usually sensitive to psychological information nor psychologically trained. Consequently, such studies are of very questionable merit when it comes to psychologizing about culture change.

Consider, first of all, what Kaplan (1961) calls the "openness and willingness to be known by others." Participant-observation provides the basic tool for "getting to know" a culture and its people, including their feelings and attitudes; the anthropological fieldworker becomes a member of the community and utilizes this status to examine various aspects of behavior from within. However much he may pride himself on the intensity of rapport he has established, his acceptance and participation and observations will depend ultimately on the complex interaction of his own personality, the openness of the culture, and the availability of accurate information concerning his subject of study. In view of this, how does one know what "his" people believe, and how does he know that he knows?

When the concern of the analyst is with culture contact stress, including the deepest feelings of the people involved, and especially when the anthropologist is "intruder" and European as well as investigator, he faces a very delicate problem. He himself may represent the cause of stress, thus changing the nature of the material made available to him. As a result, he may develop hypotheses or beliefs about culture change which stem from personal, noninclusive, and misleading experiences. For example, a six-foot-tall white American, when interviewing New Guinea natives, towers over them whether standing or sitting. He is, sometimes at least, seen in a house (his own) filled with mysterious machines and esoteric goods which the natives can neither understand nor possess. He represents other Europeans, many of whom they have every reason to distrust and fear. There is little that the investigator can do about this, no matter how much he might try. Under these circumstances, it is not too difficult to understand why the native being interviewed might feel inferior. Likewise, it is not too hard to understand why under these circumstances a native might confess his inferiority or his uneasiness, particularly if the investigator is asking him to perform a task with which he has no experience, such as working a puzzle or telling his life story in chronological order. Generally speaking, in any interaction with Europeans, a New Guinea native will admit either to his insecurity or inferiority or both or will suggest such feelings by his demeanor. This does not mean, however, that you can generalize to the group as a whole, to other contexts, or to other individuals.

In addition, the European investigator (in New Guinea, for example), if he does not completely isolate himself from all of his own kind, will soon be ex-

posed to the attitudes of other Europeans toward natives. He soon learns that there is broad agreement over the fact that *kanakas* are not as good as whites, they are "dirty," "honest," "lazy," "ignorant," and so on. As there is virtual consensus on this point, it is all too easy to be influenced by it, if only by a kind of pernicious intellectual osmosis.[2]

Lastly, somehow "it just seems reasonable" that natives "ought to feel inferior" under the usual circumstances of culture contact. Europeans have guns, power, wealth, medicine, and good food. They are larger, control machinery, read and write, and so on and on. There is, of course, some reason for supposing that when one is relatively poor or powerless, small in stature, or relatively uninformed he must feel inferior and, so the reasoning goes, natives being powerless, and so forth, must feel inferior. This, coupled with the fact above that almost all Europeans insist that natives are inferior, the same admission by the natives themselves in the context that I have defined, as well as their coveting of *some* European goods, mainly material and technological, makes it almost inevitable that we should come to the belief about inferiority stated above. This is a very dangerous form of overgeneralization at best.

If much of the anthropological data on culture change is historical, and thus unsuitable for framing psychological hypotheses respecting change, and if the typical anthropological accounts using standard interviewing and observational techniques are likewise unsuitable, what data are left from which to attempt psychological generalizations? The answer is cross-cultural psychological testing. Kaplan has indicated that in the past two decades there have been as many as 150 studies done in seventy-five societies (1961:235). It would seem that with psychological instruments of this kind, mainly projective techniques, one could assess the psychology of natives. Unfortunately it is not that simple. As it is well known (Lindzey 1961; Henry 1961; Preston 1964; Langness and Rabkin 1964), but usually underemphasized, such tests, because of the nature of the stimulus objects and the scoring categories, are very seriously loaded toward eliciting pathology. That is, they tend to produce themes or concepts such as unhappiness, loneliness, conflict, frustration, inadequacy, and so on; thus they reinforce the over-all picture of native inferiority one gets from elsewhere while at the same time allowing for few responses of a positive nature. As an example of this, let us look for a moment at a recent monograph on the testing of Alaskan Eskimos.

Caroline Preston, a psychologist with many years of experience in the field of psychological testing, writes the following in her study of Eskimos:

> How often in using these particular T.A.T. cards I have had the experience with subjects in our own culture asking me plaintively, "Don't you have any happy pictures?" Certainly these cards are designed to militate against superficial or innocuous fantasy material in the story responses . . . however, I am surprised at the frequency with which our people are able

---

[2] In all fairness, it should be made clear that not all Europeans residing in New Guinea subscribe to this view of natives but it is unfortunately a very common view among many.

to ignore or to deny the potentialities for tragedy in their story responses (1964:392).

In an attempt to clarify the situation, Preston then constructed a four-fold typology which permitted her to rate an "unhappy" situation with either "happy" or "unhappy" feelings and a "happy" situation similarly. The particular classifications of "happy" and "unhappy" were suggested by the Eskimo test results themselves. This is a worthwhile attempt to compensate for the loading toward pathology. Even after doing this, however, she found that "tragic" stories outnumber "innocuous" ones two to one, and "unhappy" feelings outnumber "happy" feelings by approximately the same proportion. Recognizing the absence of any norms with which to compare her results, Miss Preston speculates that the result may be due to: (1) Eskimo attitudes toward whites; (2) depression brought about by the practical realities of Eskimo life, or a related factor; (3) fatalism in Eskimo personality. Whereas any or all of these interpretations may prove to be correct, as Preston notes, one cannot escape the fact of the overwhelming bias toward pathology.

When you couple the "unhappy" nature of the stimulus cards in the case of the T.A.T. with the additional possibility of scoring bias, the situation appears even worse. That is, there is a tendency to score certain responses involving sexuality and aggression as pathological, or at least undesirable, whereas in another cultural context these responses may have quite a different meaning. Thus a group of natives less inhibited about these matters than we are would tend to be seen in an even more unrealistic pathological light, even when responding in a healthy, honest, and straightforward manner.

A more meaningful and finer theory of change can only be constructed on the basis of the intensive analysis of a very large number of individual cases. In so far as psychological testing is so very limited, along with the more traditional anthropological approach, the life history offers the best method for obtaining the required data. They would need to be analyzed as to the personality types involved in change, their motivational set, their feelings and attitudes toward Europeans and the contact situation and the meaning that it has for each individual. Anything less than this can only be a superficial and very broad treatment of social and cultural data involving questionable assumptions about individual psychology. In spite of this, the trend has been more toward psychological testing and supplemental information, a point we will return to again.

Personality

It is somewhat difficult to understand, especially in view of the influence of Kardiner, why analyses of individual personalities have not been forthcoming. It would seem clear that for any psychological or psychocultural analysis, interpretations of personality would be prerequisite and, for an adequate personality sketch, a life history would be necessary. However, culture-and-personality scholars did not turn to life history taking. This is due most importantly to the fact, as

Spiro has made clear, that the culture-and-personality school did not truly shift to a study of the individual in the way most usually supposed. The shift was, rather, from a traditional focus on culture as *explanandum* to culture as *explanans* and in the substitution of personality as *explanandum:*

> Indeed, even a cursory examination of the early literature of culture-and-personality will reveal how false is the claim that culture-and-personality was —or is—a "study of the individual in culture." Although some autobiographies were collected, the autobiography was exploited to the end of discovering not individual differences, but cultural influences on the individual. The "individual" was of concern not on those characteristics which differentiated him from other individuals in his group—not, that is, as an idiosyncratic person—but as a social person, as an example of a culturally molded psychological or personality type. The question to be examined was how this individual viewed as a prototypical Hopi or Samoan or Alorese acquired a Hopi, rather than an Alorese or Samoan personality. Culture-and-personality students became, in short, the personality psychologists of primitive societies—comparative human psychologists—attending always to the crucial importance of culture for personality: its development, its structure, and its functions. And since there were many new theories to be tested, culture-and-personality studies were, from their inception, strongly theoretical—if not always systematic—in orientaion (Spiro 1961:465).

One sees here the persistence of the interest in culture so manifest in the early work of Radin and carried down to the present. Here again, although one might well argue that life histories could be more valuable than other data, they are not mandatory. If you wish only to explain personality as determined by culture you turn first to descriptions of culture, descriptions not themselves the product of life history taking. In this type of research you might use life histories as a way of learning about personality, but you would not necessarily need them to learn about culture. As it is much less difficult and time consuming to use psychological tests than to take intensive life histories, as most anthropologists are not well trained in interviewing and life history taking, anthropologists have not shown interest in the individual per se and have neglected the use of life histories.

It would seem clear, however, that data from psychological testing are not of the same order as the life history and therefore the one cannot be adequately substituted for the other. Not all of either the personality or the behavioral variables or both that are investigated have been described by psychological testing, of course. They are more often defined in the same way the anthropologist has described the culture, namely, through the standard procedures of observation and interrogation; that is, knowing a little bit about a lot of people. This is clearly not a satisfactory way of assessing a personality even assuming that it is a satisfactory way of learning about a culture. The danger lies in taking units of individual behavior out of the context of the whole lives of the subjects and assuming they are comparable. The fact that many individuals behave in similar ways in similar situations may establish a culture pattern but it does not necessarily establish similar personalities, similar motivations, and similar meanings in all of the actors. It also says nothing of the deviants, who seldom get mentioned when using this procedure.

This has special relevance to cross-cultural studies of personality using the Human Relations Area Files.[3] Even if one assumes the cultural data recorded are valid—and objections can be raised to this because of their uneven quality and the lack of knowledge about exactly how they were gathered—there is little reason to assume that statements about personality are equally valid. There is no reason to suppose that because anthropologists can define culture patterns they are necessarily equally competent to define personality variables. This is not to say that they often offer specifically psychological data. The usual procedure is simply to infer the psychological dimension from the cultural facts presented. This is true also of a large number of culture-change studies as we have noted above. Thus, feelings of *inferiority* are inferred from the fact of culture contact (Langness and Rabkin, 1964), oedipal conflict is inferred from the long post-partum sex taboo, as is castration anxiety (Stephens 1962), although there is seldom, if ever, any evidence that any given *individual* in the society in question had any of these problems. One cannot deny the correlations reported between cultural variables by those who have done cross-cultural research using the files, but one can wish that there was more substantial clinical evidence to substantiate the theoretical framework, evidence which can best be obtained through the life history.

What I have said to this point applies to anthropology and culture-and-personality studies as they have developed to the present. It has been possible, although I do not think desirable, to work with relative indifference to intensive life history data. Before going on to the future of anthropological research there are some potential uses of life histories that have not been well developed and which need to be mentioned.

Role Analyses

The concept of role offers a useful approach to the anthropologist as well as to the psychologist or sociologist. Role analysis has not often been attempted by anthropologists, however, a fact that may or may not be related to the neglect of the life history method. The analysis of a life history, with its accounts of interaction with others, attitudes toward the roles played, rationalizations for either accepting or rejecting certain roles, and the number of roles played by a given individual, would be a most effective way of getting at the relationships between members of the group as well as at problems of motivation. A role, being a behavior pattern accompanying a status, could easily be analyzed out of a life history and compared with the behavior patterns of others in the same status. In so

---

[3] The Human Relations Area File is an inventory of cultural materials which are indexed and categorized according to *The Outline of Cultural Materials*. It is possible, using the Outline, to look up material on all facets of culture. The references used for the different cultures are rated as to reliability and are constantly brought up to date. Fifteen universities in the United States have such files.

far as a culture must provide roles for the attainment of desirable goals and personality must provide drives which are satisfied by performing the available roles, role provides the concept through which the interests of culture and personality intersect and is a natural area for life history research.[4]

Factors of Chance and Accident

There are many factors of chance and accident that must be taken into account when discussing human behavior and culture. Anthropologists, for example, seldom mention individuals when analyzing and discussing culture and culture change. They also frequently pay lip service only to the many idosyncratic factors involved as well as to the "great man" theory of history, as these cannot be easily discounted. There can be little doubt that many things would have occurred differently if not for the presence of some particular individual who serves as an inspiration or leader for the others. The presence or absence of such persons, as well as their effect upon the situation, cannot be predicted from a knowledge of the social and cultural facts involved. The many accounts of "nativistic" movements, "cargo cults," and similar instances of dramatic change often clearly illustrate the importance of a particular individual who acted as catalyst.[5] Life histories of such people are not always obtainable, especially "after the fact," and, when they have been, they have often been inadequate to offer many insights into the personalities of such individuals. We are loathe to admit factors of chance into our scheme of things as they are by definition "unscientific," but no theory of change can be complete without taking cognizance of such factors; there is no other way to study them except through hundreds of individual cases.

Values

In recent years there has been increasing interest in the study of values but as in the field of culture change, the tendency has been toward psychological testing and supplementary interviews rather than toward the use of the life history. Indeed, at least one new test has been designed specifically for the purpose of measuring values (Goldschmidt and Edgerton 1961). Even though life histories have been collected by students of values few, if any, have found their way into print. Not many attempts have been made to demonstrate the effect of cultural values upon the individual although the ones which have been made are very worthwhile (Adair and Vogt 1949; Vogt 1951). Part of this neglect is doubtless due to the concentration on the controversy over the study of values in

---

[4] See Spiro (1961) for an account of the crucial importance of the concept of role in culture-and-personality research. L. Spindler (1962) applies role constructs to autobiographies of Menomini women.

[5] See, for example: Burridge, 1960; Jarvie, 1963; Linton, 1943; Voget, 1956; and Wallace, 1956.

the first place—definitions, classifications of values, and the philosophical impli-cations of studies of values by anthropologists.

As one of the major problems in the study of values has to do with the discrepancy between what is believed *ought to be the case* and what in fact *is the case,* it would seem obvious that studies of many individuals are in order. Be-cause this is a very difficult procedure involving many exceptions and masses of data, scholars have tended to stick to the abstracted versions of cultural values specifying what ought to be the case as validated by a majority of verbal re-sponses or group consensus. It is very unfortunate that we are so bound by the limitations of time and space. Even so, there is no good replacement for the use of many individual cases in depth; generalizations are dangerous in the field of values just as they are in the field of culture change when they are based upon less than intensive personal accounts.

Socialization Studies

The interest in socialization has grown rapidly in the past few years and is a good area in which to use the biographical approach. The problem of how culture is acquired—involving a knowledge of learning, motivation, and reward, as well as other psychological phenomena such as attitudes and affect—can best be approached through individual cases. This method has probably been followed by students of socialization and personality formation much more than is appar-ent in the published materials, but here the tendency has been to gather and ana-lyze only selected data bearing on child training rather than to make use of the complete life history. Kluckhohn's comment that there will be little information about the first four years of age (1945:136) need not be the case as is indicated in a very interesting approach to baby biographies by Joseph Church (n.d.). Church's study includes having mothers record biographical information in detail about their infants during the first few years of life. And, although this is a dif-ficult procedure with illiterates, it is not impossible and is of course quite feasible in any area where women are literate.

Current Trends in Anthropology

John Honigmann notes that there has been a diminishing enthusiasm for culture-and-personality research since the thirties and forties, and he attributes this to the fact that new problems in social structure and linguistics have tended to draw graduate students away from this approach. He also attributes the disin-terest to the growing climate of empiricism and operationalism in the scientific community (1961:125). This does appear to be the case and has undoubtedly also affected the interest in life history materials. It is a continuation of the objec-tion to introspective data by Boas quoted earlier. Much of the criticism leveled at scholars interested in culture-and-personality has to do with the fear that anthropologists were turning away from the culture concept and toward psychological problems (Meggers 1946). Be this as it may, there is no question that there has been a revolution in anthropology in the past few years. Contemporary anthropology, whatever else it may be, is definitely theoretically inclined and no longer merely descriptive in its aims. The dichotomy between culture and individual, and hence between anthropology and psychology, has broken down and psychological variables currently are an integral part of anthropological research. The degree to which any given anthropologist admits them is, however, a matter of personal choice and interest. Anthropologists continue to be interested in studies of culture change, values, socialization, personality, and so on—studies which could be measurably improved by the use of more intensive data on individual persons. An anecdote given by Honigmann reveals the dilemma which so often confronts the ethnographer:

> Recently I listened to a discussion concerning two variant interpretations of the same data from an American Indian community. The anthropologists agreed on the facts, but they disagreed when it came to ascertaining their psychological meaning for the Indians. *For one thing, the researchers probably did not really know the people very well** and hence were handicapped for interpreting their data. They also lacked a sufficiently powerful theory in which they believed enough to apply it to their facts (1961:127).

Too often we simply do not know the people well enough, a problem of some importance if the interest is exclusively in culture but an absolutely crucial problem if the interest is in any way psychological or psychocultural. Most if not all of the problems of current interest mentioned above have a psychological dimension, and their analysis is drastically handicapped if the psychological factors are not considered along with the social and/or cultural.

This is just as true when it comes to problems of social structure, although I have not discussed them, as it is for the other problems mentioned above. Talcott Parsons and other theorists have insisted upon the mutual relevance of culture, social system, and personality for any adequate understanding of human behavior (Parsons 1961). Spiro has argued most cogently for the necessity to distinguish motive from function in explanations of sociocultural phenomena and for the necessity to distinguish social functions from psychological ones (1953, 1961a, 1961b) in the analysis of social structure and other cultural phenomena.

We have seen that the traditional anthropological interest has been in culture. When anthropologists turned to personality and psychological variables they did not turn to an interest in the individual *qua* individual but to the individual as a modal representation of one culture. The emphasis on the *individual* or *personality* involved was only lip service, as Spiro has indicated. Whereas formerly culture was the overriding interest of anthropologists and the attempt was to describe culture and its evolution and diffusion, when the "revolution" occurred, culture still remained the key concept and, as an independent rather than depen-

---

* Italics not in original.

dent variable, could be called upon to explain personality and personality variation cross-culturally. Neither the original interest in culture nor the subsequent interest necessitated the use of life history data as we have seen, regrettable as this may be. However, if the important reorientation of culture-and-personality studies suggested by Spiro, or any approximation of it, should come about, it will not be possible to continue neglecting such data. That is, if we change the focus back to culture as *explanandum,* using personality as *explanans,* and focus our emphasis on personality and personality derived concepts as our central analytic tools, it will become mandatory to take detailed, accurate and sensitive life histories. If it can be accepted that

> . . . cultures and/or social systems do not lead an independent existence of their own; that their operation and maintenance are dependent to a marked degree on their internalization (either as cognitive or as affective variables) within the personalities of the members of society. . . . (Spiro 1961:486)

and if

> . . . institutions provide culturally approved and/or prescribed means for the satisfaction of personality needs, and these, in turn, provide the motivational bases for the performance of the members of society. . . . (Spiro 1961:486)

then the life history offers the best if not the only method which will enable us to gather the kinds of data we will need. Honigmann puts the case very simply:

> Motivation and culture are not isomorphic. Motives must be assessed through studying living individuals in depth using clinical methods (1961: 99).

Current trends in culture-and-personality research do seem to reflect an increased interest in motivation. Most other trends, even though they do not necessarily deal with motivation per se, do accept psychological data as a part of anthropology. Even scholars who consciously reject psychological data as irrelevant to structural or other analysis almost invariably find it necessary to resort to some psychological concepts in their work whenever they attempt to get beyond mere descriptivism. This fact would seem to recommend the use of *biographical data* by social and cultural anthropologists whether they consider themselves scholars of culture-and-personality or not. The problems of current anthropological investigation demand a reorientation of methodology to keep pace with the shifts in interest, and this reorientation must be in the direction of more sensitive insights into the individual actors. There would seem to be at present no adequate substitute for the life history.

3

Collection of Field Data

I N THIS CHAPTER I wish to deal with the problems involved in actually collecting data in the field as opposed to those problems which arise when one
attempts to analyze such data. This is not an easy distinction to deal with as
there are many ways in which the one is intimately related to the other. This will
become clear, I think, as we proceed.

Rapport

There are probably as many problems in establishing rapport as there are
fieldworkers and fieldwork situations. Each ethnographer is in some respects a
unique personality in a unique setting and must be able to adjust to the reactions
his presence brings about in those he wishes to study. Initial contact can be of
critical importance and is often a very difficult situation. This is true whether the
group to be studied is an isolated New Guinea tribe with no previous contact
with outsiders or highly urbanized subculture of the United States which has
been subjected to an endless variety of researchers, social workers, parole officers,
Indian agents, and the like. Initial contact is difficult mainly because one must be
both cautious and bold at the same time, and also because, in spite of whether it
is objectively true or not, one usually believes that success or failure depends
upon first impressions. The fact that this is seldom true does not allay the feelings of anxiety, inadequacy, and trepidation the budding fieldworker experiences
at this time. Many techniques or "gimmicks" have been used to establish rapport.
When working with "primitives"[1] it has been traditional to offer inexpensive gifts
in the form of beads, mirrors, knives, and so forth. More recently it has also been

---

[1] I use the term *primitive* only because it has been used so widely in anthropology
that the meaning is fairly clear. I do not, of course, imply inferiority of any kind but
merely the lack of certain features usually associated with Western-European "civilization."
See Redfield, 1953.

found useful to take a polaroid camera or a tape recorder, both of which offer dramatic but usually highly appreciated diversions and quickly help to cement friendly relations.

One of the time-honored explanations for what one is doing and thus gaining access is that you wish to learn the language. As all fieldworkers should make some attempt in this direction, this is not a false claim and does act as a convenient way of establishing relations and breaking down hostility and suspicion. It is hard to perceive someone as hostile or threatening when you can laugh with him at his own mistakes when trying to pronounce foreign words and phrases for the first time.

Generally speaking, it is more difficult to establish rapport with more acculturated groups such as most contemporary American Indians and urban subcultures, and obviously the techniques just discussed cannot be used.[2] In these cases it is usually a question of caution, perseverance, and patience along with repeated displays of good faith. Offers of money or other forms of remuneration, although often made as an incentive for performing some task, have little to do with establishing rapport and indeed in most instances would be out of place. It is interesting that ethnographers who have taken life histories successfully almost universally deny that their informants were motivated by material reward. Quite often it is reported that they were just friends or were adopted kinsmen. We will return to this point later. It seems clear, however, that there is no substitute for an honest attempt to explain precisely who you are and what it is you wish to do irrespective of the level of development of the people among whom you are working. Honesty is apparently understood at a level independent of the content of the particular communication.[3]

The role of the fieldworker is of great importance here. That is, is he purely participant observer and thus virtually "one of them" or is he the mysterious, powerful, and awesome stranger? There have been differences of opinion on this score in the past, but here one does not always have a choice and the question may be more academic than real. A European fieldworker in the New Guinea Highlands, for example, no matter how hard he may try can never truly become a genuine member of the native community. This does not mean that he cannot be adopted by someone, called by a kinship term, and invited to participate in certain of the group activities. It means simply that the gap between his own culture and that of his subjects, plus his visibility, status, and knowledge, are too great to be surmounted; this would be true no matter how long he might stay in the field. Adapting to a steady diet of sweet potatoes supplemented periodically by badly cooked pork, living in an environment where there are no conceptions of personal hygiene as Western-Europeans know them, and the limited extension of certain moral prescriptions about brutality and killing are too much to ask for the

---

[2] There are exceptions to this rule, naturally. Evans-Pritchard's well-known difficulties with the Nuer (1940) is a good case in point. I know of one case in New Guinea where the anthropologist was told quite flatly that he was not wanted.

[3] Again, there are exceptions. For example, if you wished to study criminals in a prison setting you would probably not explain your intentions in advance. For a good discussion of the ethical problems involved in fieldwork see Barnes, 1963.

relatively meager ethnographic facts one would return with after a period in the field.

I do not mean to imply by this that the investigator should try to reform or change the people he is working among, or that he should betray any disgust or repugnance; it is simply not realistic to expect too much and virtually impossible to "go native." The degree to which a fieldworker will be able to participate in the native culture will vary widely depending upon his temperament, his motivation, his physical skills and visibility, and the length of time he spends in the area. There have been instances recorded in which the anthropologist has gone to what would be considered extreme lengths by most others. Alan Holmberg's privations while working with the Siriono are an excellent example (1950). At times he found it necessary to subsist on palm cabbage, nuts and fruit, and he often ate at night so as to avoid being disturbed by the perennially hungry people he followed on the march for game. While it is not usually necessary to go to the same lengths Holmberg did, it should be clearly understood by all anthropologists-to-be that the fieldwork situation calls for great tolerance. It is not unusual for natives to try deliberately to take advantage of one if only to see how much they will be permitted. It is more common for them to exasperate the fieldworker by repeated but not consciously mischievous demands for medical attention, gifts, help of one kind or another, and other kinds of attention. Naturally, the fieldworker should help, but there are limits. I know of one case in New Guinea where people would walk long distances past the medical aid station in order to receive less adequate medical attention from the anthropologist. This can be very time consuming and frustrating and obviously there are times when it is necessary to set limits even though it may be difficult at first.

It is a truism in anthropology that the fieldworker should not identify too closely with his subjects—"his people"—to a degree that it affects his scientific objectivity. It is possible to be too close to your subject matter even though you cannot completely cross the cultural boundaries and thus to be blinded to that which is obvious even to others who do not know the people so intimately. Frank Cushing, it is reported, became so involved with the Zuni that he eventually refused to publish any further accounts of them (Paul 1953:435). It is also possible, however, to be too aloof and thus to impair your work in the opposite direction. In this context it is important not to isolate yourself from the village life, either by the location of your house or by your personal habits and so on. It is just as possible to be "too clean" in the field as it is to be "too dirty."

There are some advantages in the role of stranger, provided it is the role of objective and friendly stranger rather than authoritarian, critic, or pestiferous interloper. By playing the role of stranger in the proper manner it is possible to be called upon to arbitrate disputes, to offer opinions on subjects of mutual interest, to act as an intermediary between the natives and some third party not so well known or trusted, and so on. Furthermore, one can sometimes use the prestige that accrues to his status if he is a member of a dominant or controlling group. It is not a good idea to "pull rank," but there are situations in which this is probably unavoidable. Natives have sometimes categorized all people from the outside as, for example, either missionaries, planters, or government workers, in which case it is difficult to create a new category even assuming that you were neither so socially nor physically visible. In the final analysis there is simply no substitute for honesty, patience, tolerance, and good humor, come what may; there is no excuse for the converse of these except, perhaps, in those cases where your subjects themselves know they are in the wrong and are obviously trying to take advantage of you.

The taking of an adequate and reliable life history involves a degree of intimacy with the informant and a knowledge of the community that comes only with good rapport. For this reason it is usually not advisable to attempt taking an intensive life history until one has been in the field for some reasonable period of time. The attention devoted to one or few individuals or the rewards offered can create envy and resentment in others. Working with female informants can be especially difficult in this respect for a male anthropologist, and it is only after one knows the people and the customs well that he is prepared to anticipate and handle any problems of this sort which may arise. Indeed, one might come to the conclusion that taking life histories is not worth the cost in time or rapport in certain situations. This appears to have been the case, for example, with many ethnographers attempting to work with New Guinea women, although problems of language and interpretation have also created difficulties. This is a most unfortunate situation, and the ethnographic material from New Guinea suffers as a result of it. My own experience in the New Guinea Highlands indicates that working with women, even through an interpreter, is not impossible, but that it does involve considerable expense in time and rapport.

There are other reasons, too, for waiting before attempting intensive life history work with one or few informants. Quite often there are village or clan factions, and it does not pay to become quickly identified with any one of the and thus become alienated from the others. The first few months of fieldwork are difficult; one is not sensitive to myriad cues sent out by the strange people he is with nor is he familiar with the hierarchy of power and influence. There are many other things to do besides taking life histories: less value-laden or conflict-laden activities as mapping gardens, counting people, and so on, and it is well to do them first.

Language

Since Malinowski emphasized and brought more clearly into focus the importance of learning and using native languages for fieldwork, it has been commonplace for most fieldworkers to try to emulate him in this respect.[4] Usually forgotten in such attempts is the fact that not everyone has the same facility for learning languages, not all languages are as easy to learn as others, and most fieldworkers do not have the same length of time to spend learning the language

[4] I say emphasized, for as Lowie (1940) pointed out, learning the language of those you worked with did not originate with Malinowski.

as did Malinowski. This situation has stimulated some scholars in the past to make rather exaggerated claims as to their language skills in the field. Margaret Mead wrote an article in 1939 in which she made clear the distinction between *learning* and *using* the native language. She pointed out that it was not necessary to learn the language in order to do competent fieldwork, and that different levels of language skills would suffice for different tasks. For example, if one is investigating swidden agriculture it is not quite as critical to learn the language as it is if the subject to be researched is native religion, magic, or conceptions of the universe and the good life. Furthermore, as would be expected, a great deal depends upon what the contact language is and how fluent any of the subjects are in it. That is, if the contact language is English, the anthropologist speaks English and a substantial number of informants speak English, there are no grave problems in communication. If the contact language is Dutch, the investigator speaks English, and only one or two natives speak Dutch, it makes more sense for the investigator to learn the native language.

In some cases there is a *lingua franca* available as in Melanesia where Pidgin English is widely spoken. Pidgin English, contrary to what many believe, is a bona-fide language (Murphy 1959). Although it has only a very limited vocabulary, it can be quite effective for most purposes. What generally happens when doing fieldwork in Pidgin is that after a time the investigator will mix many native words, especially nouns, with the Pidgin, which aids measurably in communication with informants. Also, if one is fortunate enough to find a good interpreter and works with him for an extended period of time, their common fund of experience makes it possible to communicate at a much higher level of understanding than would otherwise be the case. Even so, it is very difficult to communicate in Pidgin at an abstract level, and it is obvious that much more can be accomplished with fluency in the native tongue. Some investigators return several times to the same location and thus over a period of years obtain fluency. This is a commendable procedure if it can be followed.

The problem of interpretation, like all other aspects of fieldwork, depends upon the location, the particular circumstances, the amount of contact, and other related factors. In some areas of New Guinea, for example, there are no Pidgin speakers at all, in some areas you may find one or two (usually young boys or young men who are not always satisfactory for the purpose), and in still other areas virtually all the males speak Pidgin with some fluency. Almost nowhere do you find many women who speak Pidgin well and even then they are sometimes too inhibited to speak with Europeans. Obviously one must work with what is available to him, but sometimes it is possible to take an interpreter from a nearby area along who can speak both Pidgin and the language of the group with which you wish to work. Taking an interpreter with you has pitfalls in that they sometimes do not get along well with the locals. Hiring your interpreter from the same group you work with creates problems also, albeit of a different order. In this latter case you may find yourself supporting not only your interpreter but all of his relatives as well. Also, you may find that for reasons of envy or factionalism, an interpreter from the group you are working with may run into resistance from the other members.

Assuming that an interpreter of ideal qualifications can be found, it does not follow that adequate life histories will always be forthcoming. Naturally, something is lost in the translation, but too much can be made of this as well as too little. The importance of what is lost depends ultimately upon what use is to be made of the material. If it is to be used as a literary production it will doubtless suffer considerably and, if it is to be used to assess personality it will suffer, but if it is to be used as raw data with respect to a series of chronological events leading up to a war it probably suffers little if at all from the translation.

There are other problems involved in working through an interpreter. It is sometimes difficult to talk to a third party about certain areas of human behavior such as sexuality, personal habits, family matters, or questions that may involve reasons for secrecy. That is, although an informant may be willing to tell you how many pigs he has he may not be willing to divulge such information to a native interpreter. This kind of problem becomes even more serious and sometimes almost impossible when trying to work with women through a male interpreter. A native male, for example, may refuse even to ask a question relating to menstruation, child birth, intercourse, or similar topics. Here again, however, one must be careful not to be ethnocentric. I found when working with one New Guinea woman that I simply could not predict with any degree of accuracy what she would discuss and what she would not discuss. The same thing proved to be true of the interpreter I was using, and thus the problems were mainly due to my own inhibitions rather than to those with whom I was working. Furthermore, this had little to do with my ignorance of the culture but had to do, rather, with the unique circumstances which motivated the two natives to work for me in the first place. As it turned out, both of them needed the prestige derived from working with me in order to avoid what to them would have been very undesirable alternatives. My interpreter had a younger brother who had been appointed as the local native policeman. This meant, for reasons we need not discuss here, that he was in charge of directing the labor of others. If my interpreter had not been working with me he would have had to follow the dictates of his younger brother. This is a situation which would have been most intolerable and shameful because of the strong emphasis on seniority and the tradition of deference on the part of younger brothers to elders. The woman I was working with was in the process of being "divorced" by her husband. He kept stalling and refused to say whether he was actually going to divorce her or not. There was great pressure from his age mates, some of whom wanted her for a wife if he did not. As she had been purchased as a very young girl and had come from a distant place where a different language was spoken, and consequently had only a dim memory of it, she had no real desire to return. At the same time she was uncomfortable because of the men who were coveting her. She solved this by identifying with me and was, in an informal but important way, under my charge. My being aware of this made it possible for me to take full advantage of the situation and this lent a certain boldness to my questioning that would not otherwise have been possible. This illustrates again the importance of knowing the culture, your informants, and the events which are going on at the time in the community.

If one has some grasp of the native language, even if it be scarcely more than a collection of nouns and phrases, it is possible to follow an interpretation with some idea of what is transpiring and how well the interpreter is sticking to the facts. A check can also be made at selected points at other times by using different interpreters and repeating questions. If the subject knows a few words of the contact language, a more direct check can be made of certain salient points as well. Certainly one should not refrain from attempting a life history because of the necessity of working through an interpreter, at least not a priori.

Interviewing

Interviewing means, essentially, the gathering of data through direct or indirect questioning. It is an indirect means of observation. The general nature of the interview is the same in all fields in which it is featured as a technique, but there are some special problems in anthropological interviewing. Not the least of these are the problems of language and rapport discussed in the preceding section. The significance of the interview situation varies widely from person to person, but it also varies cross-culturally. Even the amount of information a person will volunteer varies widely and some people talk much more and much more freely than others. The first Clallam[5] informant I worked with, after asking me if I was going to vote for Nixon, talked almost uninterruptedly for two hours. Some of the New Guinea people never answered more than a barely audible yes or no. Kaplan reports extremely wide variation in the amount of responses given to projective test cards (1961:246).

The significance attached to an interview by a New Guinea native who does not comprehend the aims of science or data collecting is much different from that of the interviewee seeking employment in a large corporation, to take an extreme example. The aim of the New Guinean is often, perhaps, to get it over with as quickly as possible so as to get back to more meaningful pursuits such as gardening or pig tending. The aim of the interviewee is to make a favorable impression. The social role assigned to the interviewer makes a great difference and thus the information given can vary greatly from situation to situation. While in New Guinea I was witness to some of the most blatant falsehoods, usually given by a native to a strange European or to the administration officers. The motives for these prevarications are usually not difficult to understand as the people have a tendency to tell strangers what they think they would like to hear, and they like to tell the administration officers that they have fewer pigs than they actually have or that they have not neglected their coffee or other cash crops. The anthropologist has a tremendous advantage because he is constantly with the people and is interacting with them more intimately over a long period of time. This association greatly increases the reliability and the validity of the information. It is difficult to sustain a web of falsehoods over a long period of time and the anthropologist has the advantage of often being able to match up statements

---

[5] The Clallam are a Northwest Coast Indian group that currently inhabits three small communities on the Olympic Peninsula.

and observations on the spot. When he cannot do this, he can use repeated interviews with the same informant over an extended period of time, constantly checking and rechecking. He can also check an interview with one person against another interviewee and thus uncover inconsistencies and fabrications. Different informants often give quite different accounts of the same thing. If it is impossible to assess objectively which account is the correct one, either through observation or consensus, the anthropologist should specify that there were such differences of opinion. Here the personal qualities of the informant become very important and this, again, indicates the necessity of knowing the people well. It should be apparent that a life history, based upon many hours spent with the same individual and upon other information about the person gathered from those who know him, is a much more reliable and valid account than are abbreviated versions.

A related matter here is the fact that often an informant will pick the anthropologist rather than vice versa. Marginal individuals, deviants, and people who are not actively participating in the daily tasks are likely to present themselves to the fieldworker. These are the individuals who have the most time to spend watching the anthropologist at work and following him around. Sometimes they make good informants but more often not, unless one is interested specifically in deviants. Although it can be tempting to work with them, one needs to be cautious of getting a dangerously idiosyncratic view of the culture and the other people. Here sampling becomes a very important issue, and the anthropologist should make every attempt to get as wide a sample of the population as he can. The "hangers-on" are important, true, but only if they do not constitute a biased sample.

Ideally, the anthropological interview should be combined with direct observations of behavior. If, for example, one wishes information about a funeral, the best method is to observe one in progress and interview the participants on the spot. There is a drawback in this approach, however; the presence of the investigator can result in a change in the normal performance of the ceremony. Perhaps the normal procedure is not followed because of the investigator's presence, perhaps an exceptional procedure is invented on the spot so that the investigator can be included as a participant. The natives may fear that their customs will be laughed at or it may be the case that they wish to perform a ritual which has been banned by the administration. For this reason, the fieldworker should always try to get verbal accounts of former ceremonies and rituals, stressing the precontact situation and inquiring directly if anything has been modified.

The interview does give information which cannot be checked by observation. Beliefs about the supernatural, traditions, genealogies, myths, dreams, and so forth, although they may be reflected in certain forms of behavior, really exist only in the minds of the actors. Likewise, when emotions and judgments are involved there can be no substitute for the interview. When the investigator is trying to assess motivations, judgments, attitudes and emotions, the interview is a direct method as there is no other. When emotions or matters of morality are involved it is often difficult to get the informant to respond at all. In situations such as this it often helps to stimulate the informants by "bullying" or aggressive questioning. Needless to say one must be careful not to go too far with this, and some anthropologists are probably more temperamentally suited for it than others.

Perhaps it is unfortunate, but as Beals has pointed out: "The student of culture cannot ignore the objective situation, but it is the subjective view that constitutes his distinctive concern" (1953:442). It is precisely for this reason that it is so important to take intensive life histories and to be sensitive to the meanings and nuances of behavior in the interview situation. An informant will often betray by a sign or gesture or by an expression that he does not really mean what he says, or that if he means it there is something further involved. It is very dangerous to accept and repeat verbal statements without specifying, at least in your own mind, the context in which you acquired the information. A female informant in New Guinea reported to me, for example, that she and everyone else disapproved of the fact that another woman was having an illegitimate child. Her demeanor, however, indicated a contrary attitude. Further questioning brought out the fact that although she was repeating what can be considered the moral rule for such behavior, she and the other women actually believed it was good for the woman to have asserted herself and to have "put one over" on the men, so to speak. It is with respect to situations similar to this that we can see why it is desirable for the anthropologist to have some knowledge of the psychiatric interview. What Harry Stack Sullivan has written of the interview is just as pertinent to the anthropologist as to the psychiatrist:

> The psychiatrist cannot stand off to one side and apply his sense organs, however they may be refined by the use of apparatus, to noticing what someone else does, without becoming personally implicated in the operation. His principal instrument of observation in his self—his personality, *him* as a person. The processes and the changes in processes that make up the data which can be subjected to scientific study occur, not in the subject person nor in the observer, but in the situation which is created between the observer and his subject (1954:3).

It is most unfortunate that anthropologists who have successfully collected life histories have never given much information as to what actually transpired in their interview situations and what their relationship to the informant was. As mentioned before, virtually without exception anthropological biographers have denied giving material renumeration but even so they do not discuss their relationship beyond the fact that they were "friends" or adopted kinsmen. There most surely are in the anthropologist-informant relationship problems similar if not identical to transference, countertransference, identification, and defense which have never been described.[6] When I was working with one Bena Bena woman there were many problems of this sort. Once, as a brief example, she reported a daydream she had which was simply that she dreamed she had slept with me, had left my house early in the morning and started back through the village. The other people began to stare at her, she said, because her skin had turned white! I am sure that many anthropologists have had similar experiences but they

---

[6] For an account of some cultural aspects of transference, see Spiegel, 1959.

do not get into the literature and their meaning is difficult to assess apart from the complete circumstances involved. A knowledge of these phenomena on the part of the anthropologist and a serious attempt to deal with them would be of inestimable value.

Obviously the anthropological interview is not directly comparable to the psychiatric interview. The relationship between patient and therapist is very well-defined, the aims similar, and the interview takes place in much the same circumstances each time. In the field it is most often necessary to take an interview when you can. It may turn out to be a crowd conversation which takes place in a garden. It may be a formal interview in the anthropologist's home. You may have to put up with hordes of screaming children, foraging pigs, and other trying circumstances.

An interview can be directed or nondirected. That is, the anthropologist may have a particular topic in mind and thus keep his informant constantly on that subject, bringing him back to it when he begins to stray. The advantage of the nondirective interview lies primarily in that it enables you to learn what the people themselves think important—or at least what they think is important to tell the anthropologist. Nondirective interviewing of New Guinea men most often results in stories of warfare and raiding as this is a focus of male interest. While it is very useful to do this kind of interviewing, particularly at first, and one can get many clues to the natives in this way, one cannot depend on this procedure alone as it tends to result in too narrow a focus of interest. The anthropologist himself can avoid omissions of cultural materials by consulting available guides such as the *Outline of Cultural Materials* (Murdock et al., 1950) and *Notes and Queries on Anthropology* (1951). As there is no similar guide for life history materials it is extremely helpful, particularly after a few sessions of interviewing, to think out in advance what kinds of material you desire and to write down questions to ask. This is truly a necessity with informants who find it difficult to introspect and recount incidents in chronological order.

It is possible to do group interviewing, and in most situations the participants stimulate each other in a very productive way. Beals (1953:44) reports some striking cross-cultural diversity, however, and there are people who, under some circumstances, do not communicate well in groups. There are obvious advantages to interviewing people alone, of course. An adult may become quite careful in the presence of a child or vice versa. A man may be inhibited in the presence of a woman. Women and children, in New Guniea at least, are very careful of what they say in the presence of men. A rather striking example of this among the Bena involves the denial by adults that children dream. When I first learned of this I asked some children nearby who all denied dreaming. Later, when I talked to children alone, they would sometimes recount their dreams to me and they made it clear that the other adults (that is, the adult natives) laughed at them and teased them if they said anything about their dreams. There is much more to this than one might suspect as dreams are regarded as omens and can be very disturbing.

The interview is probably the most crucial single act the anthropologist in the field engages in, and much of his success depends upon how skillfull and perceptive he is in the interview situation. The student should prepare himself for this by taking practical course work in interviewing and working, if possible, with a wide variety of informants. There are many good works available on interviewing, particularly on psychiatric interviewing, and time spent with them will pay off in rich dividends in the field.[7]

Reliability and Sampling

We have only briefly touched on reliability and sampling in data collection. It might be helpful to go into some further detail. The longer the anthropologist has in the field, whether in one period or by returning several times to the same place, the greater is the likelihood that his data will be reliable. Although there are different ways of checking the verbal information received, probably the best test of reliability is simply the ability to predict accurately what people will do in a given situation and to understand what is happening. If the fieldworker's information is reliable, he will be able to get around comfortably in the culture, to avoid errors and *faux pas,* and to elicit predictable responses from the individuals he interacts with. That is to say, people will do what the fieldworker, on the basis of his data, thinks they will do. When this occurs, it confirms the working hypotheses about the culture which the investigator is constantly formulating and revising. When a predictable response does not occur, either the previous information was unreliable, or there are previously unknown conditions operating which will need to be considered.

There are three techniques for checking the reliability of anthropological data as it is accumulated in the field. The first of these is observation. If, for example, you have never seen a funeral but have had one described to you, and then you do witness one, it is possible to check your description against what actually occurs. My own experience in New Guinea indicates that verbal descriptions are usually fairly accurate but that many details are simply omitted. This is not because of dishonesty on the part of informants but simply because it is difficult to give a detailed account of this kind from memory. The observation of the event not only confirms the reliability or unreliability of previous information but it fills in details and should, as well, make sense.

Another way of assessing the reliability of information is by checking the account of one informant against another. If you are attending a ceremony and are told that a particular act of magic is performed to "make the pigs grow," it makes sense for you to move among the crowd asking several people the same question. When doing this, you might receive somewhat different answers from different people. If so, you must take into account the age and sex of the informants, their social position, their relationship to participants in the ritual, and so on. Quite often, for example, children will give different explanations than

---

[7] Highly recommended is Sullivan's *The Psychiatric Interview,* 1954. See also: Harvey, 1938; Lasswell, 1939; Nadel, 1939; Reckless and Selling, 1937; Hyman, 1951; Merton and Kendall, 1946; Rogers, 1945; Ruesch and Bateson, 1951; Ruesch, 1952; and Sheatsley, 1951.

adults, usually because of their imperfect knowledge of their culture. The consistency of response is an index of the reliability of the information. A third way, as has been mentioned before, is to ask the same questions of the same informant repeatedly over a long period of time. It is not necessary to be impolite or skeptical, but it pays to repeat. Often you can do this by pleading your own ignorance. You might say, for example, "I know you told me this before but I still don't understand it well," or "your ways are difficult for me to understand, tell me once more about such-and-such."

There is no reason to suppose that anthropological data is intrinsically more unreliable than sociological or psychological data from the investigator's own culture, except in so far as rapport and language constitute special problems and provided, of course, there has been a proper sampling of the population in question. It is with respect to sampling that doubts sometimes arise in the minds of nonanthropologists and anthropologists alike. It is all too easy to settle down in the field with one major informant or interpreter and base your work mainly on what the one person reported. Not all people in a culture are as easy to work with or are as fluent as some. A comfortable relationship with one or few informants is easier than the discomfort of working with those persons you do not like or trying constantly to form new relationships. Even so, one should try very hard to get an adequate sampling of age, sex, and social position. This means much more than just working with all the people in *some* capacity. That is, it is not sufficient that you have talked to a variety of people during the course of your fieldwork—you must also have talked to them about the same things. If, for example, there is a belief in ghosts, you should know how women feel about them as well as men, how children perceive them as well as adults, what deviant individuals think about them, and what the community leaders think about them. It is only with respect to given topics that sampling becomes pertinent. It is true that certain subjects belong predominantly to one category of person, menstruation, for example. But it is equally important to learn what, if anything, men think or know about it. The ideal situation is one in which identical questions have been asked of a completely representative sample of the population. The sum total of this would be a collection of detailed life histories which, from their idiosyncratic materials, would contain the feelings, attitudes, knowledge, and beliefs of the sample on the broadest range of culture. In practice this is difficult to obtain, but the fieldworker should be very careful not to restrict himself to too few informants and an inadequate sample.

Supplemental Data

All data on a given individual are a part of his life history. I wish to distinguish here, however, between the simple questioning and verbal exchange which goes on in the two party interview and information from other sources. Other sources means such things as reports about the individual from others, psychological testing, a medical history if one happens to be available, or any other kind of information that one might obtain.

Projective testing, although no substitute for an intensive life history, can be a valuable adjunct to the life history, particularly when comparisons with other individuals are intended. Psychological testing, other than those tests of the "projective" variety, have not been popular with anthropologists mainly because they have proven to be "culture bound." The projective tests (mainly the Rorschach, Thematic Apperception Test, Free Drawings, Doll Play, and the Bender Gestalt), being usually a series of standardized stimulus objects, offer more comparable results than the more nonstandardized interview. A further advantage of testing is that it allows the anthropologist to get at least some personality data on a larger number of individuals than he would otherwise be able to accumulate in the relatively short space of time usually allotted to fieldwork. The tests are short, relatively easy to administer, and can be analyzed by persons other than the fieldworker. One must be cautious, however, not to take this procedure for more than it is actually worth. The tests, even the best of them, do not measure personality-as-a-whole. They are of very limited utility for personality assessment apart from intensive life history data from other sources. Kaplan has written of this:

> The first assumption, for example, that the projective test samples adequately the personality processes of the individual in whom one is interested is an extremely hazardous one. There is ample reason to believe from intensive studies of individuals using many techniques (Murray 1938), or from studies of successive administrations of a single test (Kaplan and Berger 1956), that the data obtained from a single test is little more than a fragment which may on occasion have some central importance but which at best is only part of the story of personality (1961:238).

Ironically enough, the use of detailed life histories has tended to fall off among psychologists, psychiatrists, and in medicine in general, just as it has in anthropology. This has been reported by Burton and Harris who attribute it to the influence of "Rogerian, Sullivanian, and other post-Freudian points of view," in which, "genetic reconstructions and overall conceptualizations of a life history are less often attempted" (1955:xi). A similar neglect has been pointed out for general medicine by Blumer (1949:3) who attributes it to an increase in the number of diagnostic aids available such as x-ray, electrocardiograms, electroencephalograms, and so on.

The most important of the projective tests, as we have discussed earlier, tend to be biased toward eliciting responses of an essentially "pathological" nature. Nonetheless, I would recommend testing of some kind if only because of the possibility of eliciting information you might not otherwise obtain. For example, when administering a TAT to an older man in New Guinea, he suddenly launched into a very detailed description of how to butcher and cook a human body. Although I might have eventually thought to ask such a question, it certainly had not occurred to me up to that time.

When taking life history data, one should always strive to get as much information from persons other than the subject as possible. In this way it is possible to pick up discrepancies between the individual's conception of himself and the conception that others have of him. It also usually enables you to obtain information concerning the subject about which he himself might be reticent. This is especially true if something of a shameful or distasteful nature has occurred in the subject's life. One male deviant personality I worked with for some time never told me that he had refused to be initiated, a fact of singular importance in his life and a source of constant embarrassment to him. When I finally learned of it from others I managed to get some of his feelings about it even though he still could not really talk about it. Individuals who are giving their life history do tend to leave out such things and they also distort them. One Clallam informant I worked with, a hunchback since birth, insisted repeatedly that he had been born normal and had fallen off a wagon when three years of age. This was a story which helped him to cope with his intense feelings of inferiority, and he refused to give it up even when faced with the contradictory statements of others who had known him since birth. It pays to be discrete in this kind of inquiry, however, and generally speaking when someone else tells you about the person you should think carefully before repeating it to the person himself. In addition to finding out from others about someone, if at all possible, it pays to keep a daily record of what the person does, and also notes about your own feelings toward the subject.

The genealogical method is a useful way of collecting information about an individual. Here, again, it pays to go into as much depth and do as much probing as possible. It is one thing to sit down with an informant and record the kinship terms he uses for various categories of kin but quite another to elicit his real feelings and attitudes towards them. Informants are usually loathe to admit that although they should love their elder brother, for instance, they actually despise him. Likewise, kinship terms involve notions of right and obligation, and a person does not always willingly admit to having failed in his kinship obligations. Anthropologists have often been criticized by others for painting too rosy a picture of the "primitive world" and this is, in part at least, a fair criticism. The anthropologist interviews his informants, collects the kinship terms, and everyone really does turn out to be a mother or father or brother or sister to everyone else. The terms imply certain kinds of behavior, usually of a benevolent character, and the real emotions and attitudes are often hidden behind a screen of defenses. The only possible attempt to penetrate these defenses is to do extensive clinical interviewing, resulting, of course, in an intensive life history.

All kinds of data are valuable for the life history. Photographs, taken in as many situations as possible, are an invaluable aid, for once you have left the field your memory fades rapidly. Tape recordings are also helpful. Items manufactured by the individual can be useful, especially if you have others to compare them with, as they can reveal personality quirks or consistencies. An inventory of the person's household can be useful as well as either accurate descriptions or maps of the location of his houses and gardens or both, and so forth. If you are fortunate enough to obtain materials in the form of a medical or prison record, you can put them to good use. If you know the individual lived in another area for a time it pays, if at all feasible, to visit there and interview people who knew him under the different circumstances. When a person is well known outside of his own group, it is valuable to get the impressions of "outsiders" who know of him.

Note Taking and Recording

The taking of notes is a very idiosyncratic procedure. There is a story of an anthropologist who wrote very large on foolscap paper and who, at the end of his fieldwork, had a ton of notes to ship home! Others prefer more modest notes, typewritten or handwritten, on cards, in notebooks, or even on scraps of paper. It probably makes little difference just how one actually records his information provided he is able to work with it later, but there are certain obvious facts of recording worth reviewing. It is important for the sake of reliability and completeness of record to write down notes as soon as possible. Preferably, one should take notes during the interview. This is not always possible either because of the awkward physical position the anthropologist often finds himself in, or because his informant is disturbed by note taking. If it is not possible to write or type notes during the interview, it is important to pause often during the day to write things down. Too long an interview, or too long an interval between interview and recording, can cause much consternation when it comes to accurate and detailed recall. As near as I can determine from the literature, most anthropological fieldworkers have had no trouble with on-the-spot note taking and the inhibition is more usually of the anthropologists own making. There are exceptions, of course.

It is also important to keep a detailed record of the context of the interview. That is, were you told something in an "unguarded moment" (Langness and Rabkin, 1964) or in a relaxed or formal atmosphere? Did you find it necessary to probe for the information or was it volunteered? Was it in the context of a group discussion or alone? Who was present? It pays also to jot down your own impressions as to what was going on, how people appeared to you at that time, and so forth. Any additional detail can be valuable later when going over your notes and trying to remember what it was like at the time and what it all meant. It can be most helpful to keep a diary or daily record in which you record your own feelings, fluctuations in mood, mental condition, the events of the day in chronological order, and anything else that strikes you as significant.

Finally, there are obvious reasons for taking notes in duplicate and mailing one copy home where it will be safe. Many anthropologists have had their notes stolen or lost them en route from the field. There is always danger of fire or some natural calamity, and it pays to be very careful with the product of a year or more of very difficult and frustrating work. It is possible to buy notebooks with carbon inserts and carbon paper and the fieldworker is well advised to do so.

Concluding Remarks

Additional Factors of Collection and Interpretation

BEFORE going on to a conclusion, there are some further important problems in the collection and interpretation of life histories that need to be
mentioned. These are problems of a slightly different order than those
discussed up to this point, but they influence the collection and interpretation of
such materials in equally important ways.

PERSONALITY OF THE INVESTIGATOR   It has often been suggested
that anthropological fieldworkers should undergo psychoanalysis before going
into the field. The purpose of such an analysis is, of course, to give the investigator insight into his own personality and thus enable him to understand better
how much of his work reflects himself and how much reflects objective reality.
Although it is not necessary to go to this extreme, it is an idea of considerable
merit; the personality of the investigator can obviously play an important role
both in the kinds of material that will be gathered and in what subsequently happens to it.

Some investigators are much better equipped in terms of personality than
others when it comes to working intimately with "exotic" peoples. One investigator may follow his subjects everywhere, share their food, allow himself to be fon-
dled and embraced and so on, whereas another may find physical contact repug-
nant and thus maintain a greater degree of social distance. This naturally affects
the kinds of data that can be gathered. Genealogies and certain other kinds of
data, for example, can be gathered by strictly formal interviewing in which it is
never necessary to lose one's "dignity." There are fieldworkers who work out a
regular schedule for interviewing and each day a selected number of informants
pass by their desk to be formally interviewed in turn. There is the great danger in
this procedure that fact will not be well separated from fantasy and, needless to
say, the observations so necessary for reliability are neglected. Another investigator, less inhibited and reserved, may enter into the activity whatever it may be

47

and find no difficulty in crawling into pig houses, delousing both pigs and himself, eating whatever is given him, and putting up with the most fantastic demands. Some fieldworkers locate their houses right in the village and become more or less integral members of the community, whereas other prefer to build some distance away and maintain more privacy. This is, of course, a personal matter, but one should be aware of his own limitations and the extent to which they limit his data.

The personality of the investigator also becomes important when attempting to report on native personality. One investigator, for instance, may report that the people are hostile and aggressive whereas a second, from a different personal background, might perceive them as perfectly "normal" with respect to their aggressivity. The interpretation of behavior is difficult enough because of the cross-cultural variations in meaning that exist, but it can be even more difficult if you have little insight into your own personality. I have heard two fieldworkers discuss identical observations of behavior in New Guinea and come to very different conclusions about it. One concluded that it was "obviously homosexual" and the other saw it as simply another manifestation of the desire shown by the people for physical contact of all kinds with each other. These kinds of observations are quite obviously affected by the personality of the investigator, and the more sensitive one is to himself and his personal biases the greater the reliability he can attach to his work.

EDITING   Life history materials are seldom the product of the informant's clearly articulated, expressive, chronological account of his life. In any case, it is not possible simply to publish your field notes. This means that a certain amount of editing must be done, and editing necessarily detract from the spontaneity, richness, and value of the material. One is seldom certain when reading a biography just how much was informant and how much was editor. It is possible to keep a record of what questions were asked and in what order the data were elicited, but this procedure does not make for easy reading, a fact that must be taken into account, particularly when commercial publication is concerned.[1]

There is always a great deal of repetition and contradiction in the data, which also must be deleted for publication, but it can be important to know at what points the subject was repetitive or contradictory. It is desirable also to know which things the subject himself believed to be the most significant, what his demeanor was while reporting certain themes, what information was gathered from others and under what circumstances, and many other things, but it is difficult to include all of this in a published version.[2] It is possible, of course, to make your field notes available to interested parties as Oscar Lewis has done, but many anthropologists hesitate to do this and become very sensitive when it come to their notes. Sometimes the notes are illegible to anyone but the recorder and making them available involves a great amount of work. Sometimes they are incomplete with much of the material coming from the investigator's memory, and

---

[1] Both Mintz (1960) and Sayres (1956) have attempted to deal with questioning, and in their works the questions asked are included.

[2] See Sayres, 1956, for an attempt to do this.

sometimes they are probably simply inadequate. This is an unfortunate situation which could be made less unfortunate if the fieldworker would record his notes with a view towards ultimately making them public. The facts of editing will remain, and one can only attempt to be as honest and thorough in his account as possible.

ANONYMITY   There are ethical problems in modern fieldwork as John Barnes has recently pointed out (1963) which were not so apparent a decade ago. The investigator always has the responsibility to protect his informants, and this is even more important when it involves an honest and detailed account of their personal lives This is not as easy as one might suspect, especially if you are the only anthropologist to work in a certain area as others will know where you worked and with whom. It is possible to use false names, of course, and even to falsify place names and times, but the informants will recognize themselves and others in spite of this. Case materials can even be distorted, provided the details altered are not significant, but this is not desirable and should be avoided if possible. Sometimes ethnographers can delay publication until after the death of the informant and thus insure some protection. It is usually not possible to get everyone who will be affected to agree to publication, and someone will invariably be disgruntled, but it is important to try to get informants to agree to the publication of their lives and to get the other people who will be affected also to agree to what is being said about them. This is still difficult in some areas, such as New Guinea, because it is not always clear as yet to the people what "publication" actually means.

Nowadays, one cannot reasonably expect that his published work will not eventually find its way back to the area in which he worked. The world is a much smaller place than it was even twenty years ago, and illiteracy is fairly rapidly disappearing even in the remotest corners of the earth. This means that informants can be easily embarrassed as can the ethnographer himself if his work turns out to be incorrect or unacceptable to the people as an account of their lives or culture. At least one Trobriander has remarked that Malinowski did not understand their system of clans and chiefs (Barnes 1963:127), and the work of others has been similarly criticized by their subjects.

As a researcher you do, of course, have an obligation to publish and to make public the fruits of your labor. It is necessary to balance this against the obligation you have to your informants. This is true no matter where you elect to do fieldwork and no matter what kind of interest you have, but it is dangerously true if you elect to do life histories and you must strive to make clear to your subject the implications of publication for his or her life. It is important that every area be left open for further research either by yourself or by others. This is not likely to be the case if you violate the confidence of informants or prepare a distorted version of their life for others. Anthropology is a sensitive business. Each investigator must be responsible to both the demands of his profession and the demands of his informants. This is not an easy task when you must combine the roles of scientist, detective, spy, friend, alien, participant, and neutral observer all into one, but therein lies one of the great challenges of fieldwork. There is no substitute for good judgment.

Conclusion

I have attempted to trace the historical development of the use of life histories by anthropologists. I have shown the shifts in interest during various periods of time. I have attempted also to indicate that in those areas of interest, where life histories have been used, they have not been exploited to their fullest. In other areas of interest, they have scarcely been used at all even though there are good reasons why they might have or even should have been. The equation of life histories with other kinds of data seems unjustified. Psychological testing, the genealogical method, the more traditional, and limited anthropological observations do not seem to be equivalents of the life history.

In the absence of intensive biographical materials, the anthropologist returns from the field with notebooks full of statements about the people and culture collected from a wide variety of informants in an equally wide variety of situations. He has usually learned a little bit about a lot of people but not very much about any one person. He has, in addition, his descriptions of what he has observed, perhaps some psychological test results, usually many genealogies, some pictures—perhaps moving pictures, items of material culture, and some tape recordings. On the basis of these materials, he will write his articles and describe the people and culture. The question one must bear in mind is, are these data an adequate substitute for an intensive life history?

The question hinges fundamentally on whether or not one accepts psychological variables within the anthropological purview, although it is not quite as simple as that. That is, as long as the interest is in *culture,* and culture as separate and distinct from the individual, something which acts on him rather than something internalized, life histories may be useful but they are not mandatory. As long as American anthropology, for example, was interested in the collection of ethnographic facts and was exclusively descriptive in intent, it made little difference, except for validity, whether your data came in little bits and pieces from several informants or in larger pieces from one informant. The aim was to get information that would help you describe the culture, what the informant felt about it, or how he reacted to it, was largely irrelevant. American anthropology in the 1920s, as we have seen, was of this kind; what is more important is that it was assiduously "objective" also. Being objective in this way meant avoiding introspective data which was universally unfashionable at the time. This can be seen very clearly in the statements of Boas:

> they [biographies and autobiographies] are not facts but memories and memories distorted by the wishes and thoughts of the moment. The interests of the present determine the selection of data and color the interpretation of the past (1943:334).

> In his [the informants] records personal likes and dislikes may also affect the presentation of events, inclusions or omissions of pertinent data. In short the tricks that memory plays us are too important to allow us to accept autobiographies as reliable factual data (1943:335).

Now, to shift to more recent developments for a moment: when the "Copernican revolution" (Spiro 1961) came about as a reaction to the theoretically sterile fashion of the early 1900s, anthropologists tended to split into two camps, British structuralism on the one hand and culture-and-personality on the other. The structuralists systematically excluded psychological data and hence were only indifferently interested in life history data; paradoxically enough, as we have seen, culture-and-personality scholars did not turn in great numbers to life history taking either. Although it has been possible to work without such documents up to this time, due to historical and theoretical considerations, much important data seem to have been overlooked. The current problems of anthropological interest, particularly the reorientation of culture-and-personality studies with its emphasis on internalization and motivation suggested by Spiro, necessitate a parallel reorientation of methodology. The demand is clearly for personality data in depth as well as for more reliable cultural data. It would appear that there simply is no substitute for the life history in this type of research. We have also seen some of the problems involved in gathering life history data in the field. There are very important implications in all of this for the training of future anthropologists.

Textbooks in anthropology, even those in culture-and-personality, seldom deal with the collection and use of life history materials; when they do, they generally equate the life history with other methods of obtaining data such as psychological testing, the genealogical method, participant-observation, or, at best, directed or nondirected interviewing. Few, if any, anthropology departments offer courses in interviewing, life history taking and/or analysis, or both. Anthropology students are not necessarily encouraged to take advantage of such courses where they are offered as, for example, in medical schools. Now, twenty years later, Kluckhohn's 1945 account remains the only major attempt to promote life history taking. Indeed, his summary statements seem to remain current with only some minor alterations. It is true that more biographies are available now, and age and sex groups are somewhat more widely represented; but with few but notable exceptions, analyses and interpretations have still only begun to appear, we still know next to nothing about how the materials were actually gathered, what transpired between investigator and informant, and annotations remain meager and mostly ethnographic in character. The published works remain predominantly literary, humanistic, and concerned with portraying culture through a more or less representative individual. The concern with the methodological problems appears to have lessened. Given this situation, it might be observed that graduate training in anthropology has not kept pace with changing trends within the field and consequently has not trained students in the necessary skills for investigation. This, in itself, may explain some of the declining interest in culture-and-personality mentioned by Honigmann.

There is a need for more highly trained investigators who will be both skilled in interviewing and life history taking as well as in personality assessment. There is implied a renewed interest in the methodological problems involved in interviewing, interpersonal communication, and biographical reporting. It is not as if behavioral scientists cannot learn and benefit from each other; most anthropology students would be amazed at the skills of psychiatric personnel in eliciting and interpreting meanings and nuances of behavior in the interview situation. They might also be appalled at the seeming lack of concern with the validity of the information which is sometimes displayed, mostly under the pretext that, "it isn't the truth of the communication that is significant but the fact that it was reported." Psychiatrists are often ignorant of the cultural dimension of their patient's communications but anthropologists are probably often insensitive to the meaning of statements to the individual. The increasing popularity of "home visits" by clinicians, family therapy, and other innovations in psychiatry testifies to their awareness of the problems of validity and culture, but what testifies to an equivalent awareness of anthropological shortcomings? The psychiatrist's relationship to his patient is well-defined, but how many anthropologists have defined for their readers their relationship to their informant, other than that they were "friends" or adopted kinsmen? There are surely interactional problems in the anthropological setting—transference, defense, and so forth—just as there are in psychiatry, but virtually no one has reported on them or reflected on what this may or may not mean.

The lack of analyses of available biographical materials is probably also related to the continued disinterest shown by anthropologists in library research. Fieldwork is the anthropological tradition—and rightly so—but this does not preclude doing library work as well. The Human Relations Area Files have stimulated library work in a very healthy manner. Perhaps it would be possible to establish a similar cross-cultural file of personal documents indexed and categorized in ways roughly analogous to the Human Relations Area Files which would complement them and perhaps add both validity and psychological depth. Kaplan's *Primary Records in Culture and Personality* (1956, 1957) is an important step in this direction which could, perhaps, be expanded. The creation of such file would result in a renewed interest in life history taking and also might stimulate more interest in the analysis of such materials. It would be equally valuable to prepare and *Outline of Life History Materials,* similar to the *Outline of Cultural Materials,* which would guide the investigator whether he be anthropologist or some other behavioral scientist, and enable him to ask the same questions of many people. This procedure, coupled with several initial hours of completely nondirected interviewing in an adequate sample of a population would result in data that would be rich in comparative content and more reliable than more limited statements. It might also shed somewhat different light on notions about culture change, cultural structure, the importance of kinship, and the many other problems of interpretation currently bound by preconceived categories and theoretical commitments.

The Human Relations Area File is an interdisciplinary tool. The creation of an interdisciplinary companion file of personal histories would be a relatively simple matter in so far as the life history is a common denominator of behavioral science, used not only by anthropologists and medical practitioners but also by psychologists, sociologists, social workers, criminologists, and historians, and to a lesser extent by economists, political scientists and others. Nonanalytically oriented investigators often complain that psychoanalytic theorists keep their data safely locked away in private files, yet thousands of medical and case histories are destroyed each year (Blumer 1949:10). Nonanthropologists criticize anthropological data on methodological grounds yet anthropologists do not furnish life histories which, as a common methodology, could be better understood by all concerned. There would be a problem of anonymity, of course, but this could be overcome.

There is the continuing bias against introspective data and the overzealous insistence on more "objective" methods. Anthropologists, above all, cannot afford to ignore the subjective and introspective as to do so would defeat the entire purpose of the discipline. Anthropological data of all kinds are difficult to obtain and are often of questionable reliability and validity, but they are all fundamentally biographical. The more they have in depth and intensity the greater are the chances for adequacy. The more that is known about the subject and the investigator, as well as the interactional situation itself, the better the data. The problem with taking life histories does not really lie in their objectivity but mainly with the fact that they are so difficult and time-consuming and require skills above and beyond those acquired during the normal course of graduate training. The compilation of a guide to life history materials and training in its use would overcome much of the reluctance of fieldworkers to attempt them.

Anthropological interests, continuing in the direction we have mentioned, would seem to require the kinds of training suggested and a resurgence of interest in the life history as a common and fundamental research tool. Interdisciplinary cooperation in improving the life history method would be of the utmost benefit to all concerned. A common pool of comparable life history data from several disciplines as well as from all cultures would provide a staggering amount of valuable data in a relatively short time, data of the most basic kind from which could be easily extracted information pertaining to common as well as specialized interests. I cannot see how it could fail to be data of superior quality, greater reliability, and higher validity than any which now exist.

References Cited

ABERLE, DAVID, 1951, The Psychosocial Analysis of a Hopi Life-History. *Comparative Psychology Monographs,* 21: 1.

ADAIR, JOHN, and E. VOGT, 1949, Navaho and Zuni Veterans: A Study of Contrasting Modes of Culture Change. *American Anthropologist,* 51: 547–60.

ALLPORT, GORDON, 1942, The Use of Personal Documents in Psychological Science. New York: Social Science Research Council, Bulletin 49.

ANGELL, ROBERT, 1945, A Critical Review of the Development of the Personal Document Method in Sociology 1920–1940. In *The Use of Personal Documents in History, Anthropology, and Sociology,* Louis Gottschalk, Clyde Kluckhohn and Robert Angell (eds.). Social Science Research Council Bulletin 53: 177–233.

BARNES, JOHN, 1963, Some Ethical Problems in Modern Field Work. *British Journal of Sociology,* 14:118–134.

BARNETT, H. G., 1960, *Being a Palauan.* New York: Holt, Rinehart and Winston.

BEALS, RALPH, 1953, Acculturation. In *Anthropology Today,* A. L. Kroeber (ed.). Chicago: The University of Chicago Press, pp. 621–641.

BIDNEY, DAVID, 1953, The Concept of Value in Modern Anthropology. In *Anthropology Today,* A. L. Kroeber (ed.). Chicago: University of Chicago Press, pp. 682–699.

BLACKING, JOHN, 1964, *Black Background: The Childhood of a South African Girl.* New York: Abalard-Schuman.

BLUMER, GEORGE, 1949, History Taking. New Haven, Conn.: Yale Medical Library. Reprinted from *Connecticut State Medical Journal.*

BOAS, FRANZ, 1943, Recent Anthropology, *Science,* 98: 311–314; 334–337.

BOWERS, ALFRED W., 1950, *Mandan Social and Ceremonial Organization.* Chicago: The University of Chicago Press.

BURRIDGE, K. O. L., 1960, *Mambu.* London: Methuen.

BURTON, ARTHUR, and ROBERT E. HARRIS (eds.) 1955, *Clinical Studies of Personality,* New York: Harper & Row.

CASAGRANDE, J. B., 1960, Preface to *In the Company of Man,* J. B. Casagrande (ed.). New York: Harper & Row.

CAUDILL, WILLIAM, 1953, Applied Anthropology in Medicine. In *Anthropology Today,* A. L. Kroeber (ed.). Chicago: University of Chicago Press, pp. 771–806.

CLIFFORD, JAMES L. 1962, *Biography as an Art.* New York: Oxford University Press.

DOLLARD, JOHN, 1953, *Criteria for the Life History.* (With analyses of six notable documents.) New Haven, Conn.: Yale University Press.

EDEL, LEON, 1959, *Literary Biography.* New York: Anchor Books, Doubleday and Co., Inc.

EVANS-PRITCHARD, E. E., 1940, *The Nuer.* Oxford: Clarendon Press

FREUD, SIGMUND, 1925, Analysis of a Phobia in a Five-Year-Old Boy. In *Collected Papers, Volume III.* London: Hogarth Press, pp. 149–289.

GOLDSCHMIDT, WALTER, and ROBERT B. EDGERTON, 1961, A Picture Technique for the Study of Values. *American Anthropologist, 63:* 26–47.

GOTTSCHALK, LOUIS, 1945. The Historian and the Historical Document. In *The Use of Personal Documents in History, Anthropology, and Sociology,* Louis Gottschalk, Clyde Kluckhohn, and Robert Angell (eds.). New York: Social Science Research Council Bulletin 53. pp. 3–75.

HARVEY, S. M. 1938, A Preliminary Investigation of the Interview. *British Journal of Psychology, 28:* 263–287.

HENRY, WILLIAM, 1961, Projective Tests in Cross-Cultural Research. In *Studying Personality Cross-Culturally,* B. Kaplan (ed.). New York: Harper & Row, pp. 587–598.

HOLMBERG, A. R., 1950, *Nomads of the Long Bow: The Siriono of Eastern Bolivia.* (Publications of the Institute of Social Anthropology No. 10) Washington, D.C.: Government Printing Office.

HONIGMANN, JOHN J., 1961, North America. In *Psychological Anthropology: Approaches to Culture and Personality,* Francis L. K. Hsu (ed.). Homewood, Ill.: The Dorsey Press, pp. 93–134.

HSU, FRANCIS L. K. (ed.), 1961 *Psychological Anthropology: Approaches to Culture and Personality.* Homewood, Ill.: The Dorsey Press.

HYMAN, H., 1951, Interviewing as a Scientific Procedure. In *The Policy Sciences: Recent Developments and Scope and Method,* Lerner, D., and Lasswell, H. D. (eds.). Stanford: Stanford University Press, pp. 203–216.

JARVIE, I. C., 1963, Theories of Cargo Cults: A Critical Analysis, *Oceanic,* 34(1): 1–31; 34(2): 108–136.

KAPLAN, B. (ed.). 1956–1957, *Microcard Publications and Primary Records.* Madison, Wisconsin: The Microcard Foundation, 2 Vols.

———, 1961, Cross-Cultural Use of Projective Techniques. In *Psychological Anthropology: Approaches to Culture and Personality,* Francis L. K. Hsu (ed.). Homewood, Ill.: The Dorsey Press, pp. 235–254.

KARDINER, ABRAM (with the collaboration of Ralph Linton, Cora DuBois, and James West), 1945, *The Psychological Frontiers of Society.* New York: Columbia University Press.

KEESING, FELIX M., 1953, *Culture Change.* Stanford: Stanford University Press.

KLUCKHOHN, CLYDE, 1945, The Personal Document in Anthropological Science. In *The Use of Personal Documents in History, Anthropology, and*

Sociology, Louis Gottschalk, Clyde Kluckhohn, and Robert Angell (eds.). New York: Social Science Research Council Bulletin 53, pp. 78–173.

LANGNESS, L. L., and LESLIE Y. RADKIN, 1964, Culture Contact Stress: Bena Bena Attitudes and Feelings as Expressed in TAT Responses and Unguarded Moments. Paper presented to the First International Congress of Social Psychiatry, London, August, 1964. To be published in Proceedings.

LASSWELL, HAROLD, 1939, The contribution of Freud's Insight Interview to the Social Sciences. *American Journal of Sociology,* 45: 375–390.

LEWIS, OSCAR, 1961, *The Children of Sanchez: Autobiography of a Mexican Family.* New York: Random House.

LINDZEY, GARDNER, 1961, *Projective Techniques and Cross-Cultural Research,* New York: Appleton.

LINTON, RALPH, Nativistic Movements. *American Anthropologist,* 45: 230–240.

LOWIE, ROBERT H. 1940, Native Languages as Ethnographic Tools. *American Anthropologist,* 42: 81–89.

MEAD, MARGARET, 1939, Native Languages as Field Work Tools. *American Anthropologist,* 41: 189–206.

MEGGERS, BETTY J., 1946, Recent Trends in American Ethnology. *American Anthropologist,* 48: 176–214.

MERTON, ROBERT K., and PATRICIA K. KENDALL, 1946, The Focused Interview. *American Journal of Sociology,* 51: 541–557.

MINTZ, SIDNEY, 1960, *Worker in the Cane: A Puerto Rican Life History.* New Haven, Conn.: Yale University Press.

MULLETT, CHARLES F., 1963, *Biography as History: Men and Movements in Europe Since 1500.* A Publication of the American Historical Association's Service Center for Teachers of History. New York: Macmillan.

MURDOCK, G. P., et al. 1950, *Outline of World Cultures.* New Haven: Conn. Behavioral Science Outlines, Human Relations Area Files.

MURPHY, JOHN J., 1959, *The Book of Pidgin English.* Brisbane, Australia: W. R. Smith and Paterson Pty. Ltd.

NADEL, S. F., 1939, The Interview Technique in Social Anthropology. In *The Study of Society,* F. C. Bartlett (ed.). New York: Macmillan.

NEWMAN, PHILIP, 1965, *Knowing the Gururumba.* New York: Holt, Rinehart and Winston.

Notes and Queries on Anthropology, 1951. *Methods and Techniques in Social Anthropology.* (6th ed.) London: Routledge and Kagen Paul, 36–62.

PARSONS, TALCOTT, 1961, Social Structure and the Development of Personality. In *Studying Personality Cross-Culturally,* B. Kaplan (ed.). New York: Harper & Row, pp. 165–200.

PAUL, BENJAMIN, 1953, Interview Techniques and Field Relationships. In *Anthropology Today,* A. L. Kroeber (ed.). Chicago: University of Chicago Press, pp. 430–451.

PRESTON, CAROLINE, 1964, Psychological Testing with Northwest Coast Alaskan Eskimos. *Genetic Psychology Monographs,* 69: 323–419.

RADIN, PAUL, 1920. *The Autobiography of a Winnebago Indian.* University of

California Publications in American Archaeology and Ethnology, 16: 381–473.

RECKLESS, W. C., and L. S. SELLING, 1937, A Sociological and Psychiatric Interview Compared. *American Journal of Orthopsychiatry,* 7: 532–539.

REDFIELD, ROBERT, 1953, *The Primitive World and its Transformations.* Ithaca, N.Y.: Cornell University Press.

REYHER, REBECCA HOURWICH, 1948, *Zulu Woman.* New York: Columbia University Press.

RIVERS, W. H. R., 1910, The Genealogical Method of Anthropological Inquiry. *Sociological Review,* 3: 1–12.

ROGERS, C., 1945, The Non-directive Method as a Technique for Social Research. *American Journal of Sociology,* 50: 272–283.

RUESCH, JURGEN, 1952, The Therapeutic Process from the Point of View of Communication Theory. *American Journal of Orthopsychiatry,* 22: 690–700.

———, and G. BATESON, 1951, *Communication: The Social Matrix of Psychiatry.* New York: Norton.

SAYRES, WILLIAM C., 1956, *Sammy Louis: The Life History of a Young Micmac.* New Haven, Conn.: Compass Publication Co.

SHEATSLEY, P. B., 1951, The Art of Interviewing and a Guide to Interviewer Selection and Training. In *Research Methods in Social Relations.* M. Jahoda, M. Deutsch, and S. W. Cook, (eds.). New York: Dryden Press, pp. 463–492.

SHIRER, WILLIAM, 1959, *The Rise and Fall of the Third Reich.* London: Pan Books Ltd.

SMITH, F., 1954, *Baba of Karo.* London: Faber.

SMITH, M. G., 1954, Introduction. In *Baba of Karo,* M. F. Smith, London: Faber, pp. 11–34.

SPIENEL, JOHN P., 1959, Some Cultural Aspects of Transference and Counter-Transference, In *Science and Psychoanalysis: Individual and Family Dynamics,* J. H. Masserman (ed.). New York: Grune and Stratton, pp. 160–182.

SPINDLER, GEORGE D., 1952, Personality and Peyotism in Menomini Indian Acculturation. *Psychiatry,* 15: 151–159.

SPINDLER, LOUISE S., 1962, *Menomini Woman and Culture Change.* Memoirs of the American Anthropological Association 64(1), Part 2.

SPIRO, MELFORD E., 1953, A Typology of Functional Analysis. *Explorations,* 1: 84–95.

———, 1961a, An Overview and A Suggested Reorientation. In *Psychological Anthropology,* Francis L. K. Hsu (ed.). Homewood, Ill.: The Dorsey Press.

———, 1961b, Social Systems, Personality, and Functional Analysis. In *Studying Personality Cross-Culturally.* B. Kaplan (ed.). New York: Harper & Row, pp. 93–128.

STEIN, GERTRUDE, 1933, *The Autobiography of Alice B. Toklas.* New York: Random House.

58 · REFERENCES CITED

STEPHENS, WILLIAM N., 1962, *The Oedipus Complex*. New York: Free Press.

SULLIVAN, HARRY STACK, 1954, *The Psychiatric Interview*, Helen Swick Perry and Mary Ladd Gawel (eds.). New York: Norton.

THOMAS, W. I., and FLORIAN ZNANIECKI, 1918–1920. *The Polish Peasant in Europe and America*. 5 vols. Boston: Richard G. Badger.

VOGET, FRED W., 1956, The American Indian in Transition. *American Anthropologist*, 58: 249–263.

VOGT, EVON Z. 1951, Navaho Veterans: A Study of Changing Values. Papers of the Peabody Museum of American Archaeology and Ethnology, Harvard University, 41(1).

WALLACE, ANTHONY F. C., 1956, Revitalization Movements. *American Anthropologist*, 58: 264–281.

WHITING, JOHN W. M., and IRVIN L. CHILD, 1953, *Child Training and Personality*. New Haven, Conn.: Yale University Press.

WOLFE, THOMAS, 1961, A Portrait of Bascom Hawke. In *The Short Novels of Thomas Wolfe*, C. Hugh Holman (ed.). New York: Charles Scribner's Sons.

Selected Bibliography
of Biographical
and Methodological Works

To 1925

ANDERSON, RUFUS, 1825, *Memoir of Catherine Brown, a Christian Indian of the Cherokee Nation*. Boston: Crocker and Brewster (2d edition).

ANONYMOUS, 1823, *The History of Prince Lee Boo to Which is Added, the Life of Paul Cuffey, a Man of Colour*. London: T. Hughes.

ANONYMOUS (SAMUEL G. GOODRICH), 1843, *Lives of Celebrated American Indians*. Boston: Bradbury, Soden and Company.

ANONYMOUS, 1872, *Memoir of the Distinguished Mohawk Indian Chief, Sachem and Warrior, Captain Joseph Brant*. Brantford, Ontario: C. E. Stewart & Company.

APES, WILLIAM, 1831, *A Son of the Forest, the Experience of William Apes, a Native of the Forest*. Written by himself. (2d ed.). New York: G. F. Bumce.

BARRETT, S. M., 1906, *Geronimo's Story of His Life*. New York: Duffield & Company.

BENNETT, G. 1883, An Account of Elau, a Malayan Papuan Child. *Austral. M. Gaz.*, 2: 255–258.

BLACK HAWK, 1834, *Life of Ma-Ka-Tai-Me-She-Kia-Kiak or Black Hawk*. Dictated by himself. Boston: Russell, Odiorne & Metcalf.

BONNER, T. D. (ed.), 1856, *The Life and Adventures of James P. Beckwourth, Mountaineer, Scout, and Pioneer and Chief of the Crow Nation of Indians*. New York: Harper and Brothers. (Also later editions).

BOURKE, J. G. The Medicine Man of the Apache. Ninth Annual Report of the Bureau of American Ethnology.

BROWN, REV. G. 1898, Life History of a Savage. *Australian Association for the Advancement of Science*, 7: 778–790

———, 1910, *Melanesians and Polynesians; Their Life Histories Described and Compared*. London: Macmillan.

CHIEF JOSEPH, 1879, An Indian's View of Indian Affairs. *North American Review*, 128: 412–433.

COPWAY, GEORGE, 1847, *The Life, History, and Travels of Kah-Ge-Ga-Gah-Bowh*

(George Copway), a Young Indian Chief of the Ojebwa Nation. Written by himself (6th ed.). Philadelphia: James Harmstead.

CUFFE, PAUL, 1839, *Narrative of the Life and Adventures of Paul Cuffe, a Pequot Indian: During Thirty Years Spent at Sea, and in Travelling in Foreign Lands.* Vernon: H. N. Bill.

CURTIS, EDWARD S., 1922, *The North American Indian. XII.* Norwood, Massachusetts: The Plimpton Press.

DRAKE, BENJAMIN, 1841, *Life of Tecumseh, and of His Brother the Prophet, With a Historical Sketch of the Shawanoe Indians.* Cincinnati, Ohio: E. Morgan & Company.

DRAKE, BENJAMIN, 1854, *The Great Indian Chief of the West: or Life and Adventures of Black Hawk.* Cincinnati, Ohio: Applegate and Co.

DRAKE, SAMUEL G. *The Aboriginal Races of North America; Comprising Biographical Sketches of Eminent Individuals, and an Historical Account of the Different Tribes* (15th ed.). New York: Hurst & Company.

DUNBAR, J. B. 1880, Sketch of Pitalesharu, Head Chief of the Pawnees. *Magazine of American History,* 5: 343–345.

EASTMAN, CHARLES A., 1902, *Indian Boyhood.* New York: McClure, Phillips & Co.

EATON, RACHEL CAROLINE, 1914, *John Ross and the Cherokee Indians.* Menasha, Wisconsin: George Banta Press.

EGGLESTON, EDWARD, and L. S. SEELVE, 1878, *Tecumseh and the Shawnee Prophet.* New York: Dodd, Mead and Co.

———, 1879, *Brant and Red Jacket.* New York.

EGGLESTON, G. C., 1878, *Red Eagle and the Wars with the Creek Indians of Alabama.* New York.

ELLIS, EDWARD S. 1861, *The Life of Pontiac, the Conspirator, Chief of the Ottawas.* New York: Beadle and Co.

———, 1898, *Tecumseh, Chief of the Shawanoes; A Tale of the War of 1812.* By Colonel H. R. Gordon (pseud.) New York: E. P. Dutton and Co.

ENIMIKEESO, 1867, *The Indian Chief: An Account of the Labours, Losses, Sufferings, and Oppression of Ke-Zig-Ko-E. Ne-Ne (David Sawyer) a Chief of the Ojibeway Indians in Canada West.* London: William Nichols.

FOSTER, GEORGE E., 1885, *Se-quo-yah. The American Cadmus and Modern Moses. A Complete Biography of the Greatest of Redmen.* Philadelphia: Office of the Indian Rights Association.

GRANT, W., 1905, Magato and His Tribe, *J. Royal Authrop. Inst.* 35: 266–270.

GRINNELL, GEORGE BIRD, 1889, *Pawnee Hero Stories and Folk Tales.* New York: Forest and Stream Publishing Co.

———, 1892, *Blackfoot Lodge Tales.* New York: Charles Scribner's Sons.

HALE, H., 1885, *The Obsequies of Red Jacket at Buffalo.* Trans. Buffalo Hist. Soc. 3.

HODGE, F. W. (ed.), 1907, *Handbook of the American Indians North of Mexico.* Washington, D.C.: Smithsonian Institution. Bureau of American Ethnology Bulletin 30.

HOPKINS, SARAH WINNEMUCCA, 1883, *Life Among the Piutes: Their*

Wrongs and Claims. Edited by Mrs. Horace Mann. Boston: Cupples, Upham and Company.

HOWARD, OLINER, O., 1881, *Nez Perce Joseph, An Account of His Ancestors, His Lands, His Confederates, His Enemies, His Murders, His War, His Pursuit and Capture.* Boston: Lee and Shepard.

———, 1907, *Famous Indian Chiefs I Have Known.* New York: The Century Co.

HUBBARD, J. NILES, 1886, *An Account of Sa-Go-Ye-Wat-Ha, or Red Jacket and His People.* Albany.

JOHNSON, W. FLETCHER, 1891, *Life of Sitting Bull and History of the Indian War, of 1891.* Edgewood Publishing Co.

JOHNSTON, CHARLES H. L., 1909, *Famous Indian Chiefs.* Boston: L. C. Page and Co.

JONES, PETER, REV., 1860, *Peter Jones, Life and Journals of Kah-ke-wa-quo-na-by: (Rev. Peter Jones) Wesleyan Missionary.* Toronto: A. Green.

KOPPERS, WILHELM, 1924, *Unter Feuerland Indianern.* Stuttgart: Strecker and Schroder.

KROBER, A. L., 1908, *Ethnology of the Gros Ventre.* Anthropological Papers of the American Museum of Natural History, War Experiences of Individuals. 1 (4): 196–222.

LEUTWEIN, THEODOR, 1912, *Die Kampfe mit Hendrik Witboi 1894 und Witbois Ende.* Leipzig: R. Voigtlander.

LINCECUM, GIDEON, 1906, *Life of Apushimata.* Mississippi Historical Society Publication, 9.

LOVE, W. DE LOSS, 1900, *Samson Occum and the Christian Indians of New England.* Boston: The Pilgrim Press.

LOWE, MARTHA PERRY, 1881, *The Story of Chief Joseph.* Boston: D. Lothrop and Co.

McWHORTER, LUCULLUS VIRGIL, 1920, *The Discards.* Yakima, Wash.

MALLERY, GARRICK, 1893, *Picture Writing of the American Indians.* Tenth Annual Report of the Bureau of American Ethnology. Washington, D.C.

MATSON, N., 1880, *Memories of Shaubena* (2d ed.). Chicago: Donnelley, Gassette and Loyd.

MEACHEM, A. B., 1876, *Wi-ne-ma and Her People.* Hartford, Conn.: American Publishing Co.

O'BEIRNE, H. F., 1891, *Leaders and Leading Men of the Indian Territory with Interesting Biographical Sketches.* Chicago: American Publishers Association.

OLDEN, SARAH EMILIA, *The People of Tipi Sapa.* Milwaukee, Wisconsin: Morehouse Publishing Co.

PARSONS, ELSIE C., 1919, Waiyautitea of Zuni, New Mexico. *Scientific Monthly,* 9: 443–457.

PARSONS, ELSIE C., 1921, A Narrative of the Ten'a of Anvik, Alaska. *Anthropos,* 16: 51–71.

PARSONS, ELSIE C. (ed.), 1922, *American Indian Life.* New York: B. W. Huebsch.

PATTERSON, J. B. (ed.), 1882, *Autobiography of Ma-Ka-Tai-Me-She-Kia-Kiak, or Black Hawk.* St. Louis: Continental Printing Co.

PIERCE, EBENEZER W., 1878, *Indian History, Biography and Genealogy: Pertaining to the Good Sachem Massasoit.* North Abington: Published by Zerviah Gould Mitchell.

POPE, SAXTON T., 1920, *The Medical History of Ishi.* University of California Publications in American Archaeology and Ethnology, 13: 175–213.

RADIN, PAUL, 1913, Personal Reminiscences of a Winnebago Indian. *Journal of American Folklore,* 26: 293–318.

RIVERS, W. H. R., 1900, A Genealogical Method of Collecting Social and Vital Statistics. *J. Royal Anthrop. Inst.,* 30: 74–82

———, 1918, Dreams and Primitive Culture. *Bulletin of John Rylands Library,* 4: 386–410.

SAPIR, EDWARD, 1921, The Life of a Nootka Indian. *Queens Quarterly,* 28: 232–243; 351–367. (Reprinted in *American Indian Life,* E. C. Parsons (ed.). New York: B. W. Huebsch, 1922.)

SCHMIDT, P. W., 1906, Die Moderne Ethnologie. *Anthropos* I: 134–163; 318–386; 592–642; 950–997.

SCHULTZ, J. W., 1907, *My Life As An Indian.* New York: Houghton Mifflin Co.

SPLAWN, A. J., 1917, *Ka-Mi-Akin, Last Hero of the Yakimas.* Caldwell, Idaho: The Caxton Printers.

STANLEY, J. M., 1852, *Portraits of North American Indians.* Washington, D.C.: Smithsonian Institution.

STONE, WILLIAM L., 1841, *The Life and Times of Red Jacket or Sa-Go-Ye-Wat-Ha.* New York: Wiley; London: Putnam & Co.

———, 1842, *Uncas and Miantonomoh.* New York: Dayton and Newman.

———, 1865, *Life of Joseph Brant.* 2 vols. Albany: J. Munsell.

THATCHER, B. B., 1832, *Indian Biography: or an Historical Account of Those Individuals Who have Been Distinguished among the North American Natives as Orators, Warriors, Statesmen and Other Remarkable Characters.* New York: J. & J. Harper.

VIERKANDT, A., 1908, Fuhrende Individuen bei den Naturvolker Zeit. *fur Social Wissenschaft,* 2: 542–554, 623–640.

WALLIS, WILSON D., 1919, *Sun Dance of the Canadian Dakota.* Anthropological Papers of the American Museum of Natural History, Vol. 16, Personal Narratives, pp. 317–381.

WATERMAN, T. T., 1918, *The Yana Indians.* University of California Publications in American Archaeology and Ethnology, 13: 35–102.

WATSON, VIRGINIA, 1916, *The Princess Pocahontas.* Philadelphia: The Penn Publishing Co.

WELCH, ANDREW, 1841, *A Narrative of the Early Days and Remembrances of Oceola Nikkanochee, Prince of Econchatti, a Young Seminole Indian; Son of Econchatti-Mico, King of the Red Hills, in Florida.* Written by his guardian. London: Hatchard and Son.

WILSON, GILBERT L., 1917, *Agriculture of the Hidatsa Indians. An Indian Interpretation.* University of Minnesota, Studies in the Social Sciences No. 9.

WILSON, GILBERT L., 1924, The Horse and Dog in Hidatsa Culture. Anthropological Papers of the American Museum of Natural History, Vol. 15, Part 2.

WISSLER, CLARK, 1922, *Smoking Star, A Blackfoot Shaman, in American Indian Life,* Elsie C. Parsons (ed.). New York: Viking.

WOOD, NORMAN B., 1906, *Lives of Famous Indian Chiefs.* Aurora, Ill.: American Indian Historical Publishing Co.

WOOD, LOUIS A., 1915, The War Chief of the Six Nations. In *Chronicles of Canada,* V. 16, Toronto, Canada.

1925 to 1944

ADLER, ALFRED, 1929, *The Case of Miss R.* London: George Allen & Unwin.

AGINSKY, B. W., 1940, An Indian's Soliloquy. *American Journal of Sociology,* 46: 43–44.

ANDERSON, EVA GREENSLIT, 1943, *Chief Seattle.* Caldwell, Idaho: Caxton Printers.

BARBEAU, MARIUS, 1928, *The Downfall of Temlaham.* Toronto: Macmillan.

BARNETT, H. G., 1941, Personal Conflicts and Cultural Change. *Social Forces,* 20: 160–171.

———, 1942, Review of *Smoke from Their Fires* by C. S. Ford. *American Anthropologist,* 44: 299–300.

BARTON, R. F., 1938, *Philippine Pagans, the Autobiographies of Three Ifugaos.* London: Routledge & Kegan Paul

BATESON, GREGORY, 1934, Field Work in Social Psychology in New Guinea. In Proceedings of the First International Congress of Anthropological and Ethnological Sciences. London.

———, 1942, Some Systematic Approaches to the Study of Culture and Personality. *Character and Personality,* 11: 76–82.

———, 1944, Pidgin English and Crosscultural Communication. Transactions of the New York Academy of Sciences, Ser. 2, 6: 137–141.

———, and MARGARET MEAD, *Balinese Character. A Photographic Analysis.* New York: New York Academy of Sciences.

BEAGLEHOLE, ERNEST, 1939, Some Modern Hawaiians: Culture and Psychosis in Hawaii, Honolulu. *University of Hawaii Publication* 19.

———, and PEARL BEAGLEHOLE, 1939, Brief Pukapukan Case History. *The Journal of the Polynesian Society,* 48: 134–143.

BEALS, FRANK L., 1943, *Chief Black Hawk.* Chicago.

BERNARD, JESSIE, 1928, Political Leadership Among North American Indians. *American Journal of Sociology,* 34: 296–315.

BILLIG, OTTO, JOHN GILLIN, and WILLIAM DAVIDSON, 1947–1948, Aspects of Personality and Culture in a Guatamalan Community: Ethnological and Rorschach Approaches. *Journal of Personality,* 16: 153–187; 326–368.

BLODGETT, HAROLD, 1935, *Samson Occom.* Hanover, N.H.: Dartmouth College Publications.

BLUMER, H., 1939, An Appraisal of Thomas and Znaniecki's *The Polish Peasant in Europe and America.* Critiques of Research in the Social Sciences, 1. New York: Social Science Research Council.

BLYTH, ALICE DUKES, n.d., A Possible Significance of Life History Material to the Ethnographer as Demonstrated by a Study of Son of Old Man Hat. Unpublished typescript of a thesis for undergraduate honors, Radcliffe College. Copy in the library of the Peabody Museum of Harvard University, Cambridge, Massachusetts.

BONNERJEA, BIREN, 1935, Reminiscences of a Cheyenne Indian. *Journal de la Societe des Americanistes de Paris,* 27: 129–143.

BRITT, ALBERT, 1938, *Great Indian Chiefs.* New York: McGraw-Hill.

CANNON, WALTER B., 1942, Voodoo Death. *American Anthropologist,* 44: 169–181.

CARTWRIGHT, DORWIN, and JOHN R. P. FRENCH, 1939, The Reliability of Life History Studies. *Character and Personality,* 8: 110–119.

CAUGHEY, JOHN WALTON, 1938, *McGillivray of the Creeks.* Norman, Okla.: University of Oklahoma Press.

CHAPLIN, HOWARD M., 1931, *Sachems of the Narragansetts.* Providence: Rhode Island Historical Society.

COLE, CYRENUS, 1938, *I Am A Man: The Indian Black Hawk.* Iowa City, Iowa: State Historical Society of Iowa.

COLSON, ELIZABETH, n.d., The Life Hisotry of Elizzie Francisco. Typescript.

COOPER, JOHN M., 1933, The Cree Wiitko Psychosis, *Primitive Man,* 6: 20–24.

DAI, BINGHAM, 1941, Personality Problems in Chinese Culture. *American Sociological Review,* 6: 688–96.

DALE, EDWARD EVERETT, and GASTON LITTON, 1939, *Cherokee Cavaliers: Forty Years of Cherokee History as Told in the Correspondence of the Ridge-Watie-Boudinot Family.* Norman, Okla.: University of Oklahoma Press.

DAVIS, ALLISON, and JOHN DOLLARD, 1940, *Children of Bondage. The Personality Development of Negro Youth in the Urban South.* Washington, D.C.: American Council on Education.

DUBOIS, CORA, 1937, Some Anthropological Perspectives on Psychoanalysis. *Psychoanalytic Review,* 24: 254.

———, 1937, Some Psychological Objectives and Techniques in Ethnography. *Journal of Social Psychology,* 8: 285–301.

———, 1939, *The 1870 Ghost Dance.* University of California Publications in Anthropological Records, 8: 1–152.

———, 1944, *The People of Alor.* Minneapolis, Minn.: University of Minnesota Press.

DYK, WALTER, 1938, *Son of Old Man Hat: A Navaho Autobiography Recorded by Walter Dyk.* With an introduction by Edward Sapir. New York: Harcourt.

———, 1947, *A Navaho Autobiography.* Viking Fund Publications in Anthropology No. 8.

EAST, R., 1939, *Akiga's Story: The Tiv Tribe as Seen by One of Its Members.* London: International Institute of African Languages and Cultures.

EASTMAN, CHARLES ALEXANDER, 1931, From the Deep Woods to Civilization. Chapters in *The Autobiography of an Indian.* Boston: Little, Brown.

ELKIN, A. P., 1941, Native Languages and the Field Worker in Australia. *American Anthropologist,* 43: 89–94.

ERIKSON, E. H., 1943, Observations on the Yurok: Childhood and World Image. University of California Publications in American Archaeology and Ethnology, 35: 257–301.

FORD, CELLAN S., 1941, *Smoke from Their Fires.* New Haven, Conn.: Yale University Press.

FOREMAN, GRANT, 1938, *Sequoyah.* Norman, Okla.: University of Oklahoma Press.

FOSTER, MRS. W. GARLAND (ANNA FOSTER), 1931, *The Mohawk Princess: Being Some Account of the Life of Tekahion-Wake (E. Pauline Johnson).* Vancouver: Lion's Gate Publishing Co.

FRANZ, G. H., 1929, *Tau, the Chieftain's Son.* Dundee, Natal.

FRENCH, THOMAS M., 1944, Clinical Approach to the Dynamics of Behavior. *Personality and the Behavior Disorders,* J. McV. Hunt (ed.). New York: The Ronald Press Co., pp. 255–268.

FRENKEL, ELSA, 1936, Studies in Biographical Psychology. *Character and Personality,* 5: 1–34.

FRENKEL-BRUNSWIK, ELSA, 1939, Mechanisms of Self Deception. *Journal of Social Psychology,* 10: 409–420.

GABRIEL, RALPH HENRY, 1941, *Elias Boudinot, Cherokee, and His America.* Norman, Okla.: University of Oklahoma Press.

GARNETT, DAVID, 1933, *Pocahontas, or the Nonpareill of Virginia.* New York: Harcourt.

GILLIN, JOHN, 1939, Personality in Preliterate Societies. *American Sociological Review,* 4: 681–720.

GOLLOCK, GEORGINA ANNE, 1928, *Lives of Eminent Africans.* New York: Longmans, Green & Co.

GORER, GEOFFREY, 1938, *Himalayan Village; and An Account of the Lepchas of Sikkim.* London: Michael Joseph, Ltd.

GRINNELL, GEORGE BIRD, 1926, *By Cheyenne Campfires.* New Haven, Conn.: Yale University Press.

HALL, CALVIN, and GARDNER LINDZEY, 1954, Psychoanalytic Theory and Its Application in the Social Sciences. In *Handbook of Social Psychology.* Lindzey (ed.). Reading, Mass.: Addison-Wesley, pp. 143–180.

HALLOWELL, A. I., 1934, Culture and Mental Disorders. *Journal of Abnormal and Social Psychology,* 29: 1–9.

———, 1938, Fear and Anxiety as Cultural and Individual Variables in a Primitive Society. *The Journal of Social Psychology,* 9: 25–47.

———, 1939, Sin, Sex and Sickness in Saulteaux Belief. *The British Journal of Medical Psychology,* 18: 191-197.

————, 1941, The Rorschach Method As an Aid in the Study of Personalities in Primitive Societies. *Character and Personality,* 9: 235–245.

HARRINGTON, M. R., 1933, The Life of a Lenape Boy. *Pennsylvania Archaeologist,* 3: 3–8.

HATT, E. DEMANT, 1931, *Turi's Book of Lappland.* London: Jonathan Cape.

HEBARD, GRACE RAYMOND, 1933, *Sacajawea, a guide and interpreter of the Lewis and Clark expedition, with an account of the travels of Toussaint Charbonneau, and of Jean Baptiste, the expedition papoose.* Glendale, California: The Arthur H. Clark Co.

HENRY, JULES, 1940, A Method for Learning to Talk Primitive Languages. *American Anthropologist,* 42: 635–641.

HENRY, JULES, and ZUNIA HENRY, 1944, *Doll Play of Pilaga Indian Children.* Research Monographs of the American Othopsychiatric Association No. 4.

HOWARD, HELEN ADDISON, 1941, *War Chief Joseph.* Caldwell, Idaho: The Caxton Printers.

HUGHES, THOMAS, 1927, *Indian Chiefs of Southern Minnesota.* Mankato, Minnesota.

KLUCKHOHN, CLYDE, n.d., The Life Story of a Navaho Indian. Typescript.

————, 1939, Theoretical Basis for an Empirical Method of Studying the Acquisition of Culture by Individuals. *Man,* 38: 89.

————, 1944, The Influence of Psychiatry Upon Anthropology During the Past One Hundred Years. In *Centennial History of American Psychiatry.* New York: Columbia University Press.

————, and O. H. MOWRER, 1944, Culture and Personality: A Conceptual Scheme. *American Anthropologist,* 46: 1–29.

KLUCKHOHN, FLORENCE, 1940, The Participant-Observer Technique in Small Communities. *American Journal of Sociology,* 46: 331–343.

KOPPERS, WILHELM, 1928, Individualforschung unter den Primitiven. In *Besonderen unter den Yamana auf Feuerland.* Vienna: Schmidt-Festschrift (W. Koppers, ed.); Vienna: Mechitharisten-Congregations, 349–365.

KREFT, H. H. G., 1926–1927, The Diary of Hendrik Witbooi. *Journal of the South West Africa Scientific Society,* 2: 49–61.

KROEBER, A. L., 1942, *Yurok Narratives.* University of California Publications in American Archaeology and Ethnology, 35: 167–171.

LANDES, RUTH, 1938, *The Ojibwa Woman.* New York: Columbia University Press.

LANGMUIR, IRVING, 1943, Science, Common Sense and Decency. *Science,* 97: 1–7.

LAUBSCHER, B. J. F., 1939, *Sex, Custom and Psychopathology.* London: Routledge and Keegan Paul.

LEE, CHESTER ANDERS, 1936, *Chief Joseph, the Biography of a Great Indian.* New York: Wilson-Erickson.

LEIGHTON, ALEXANDER, and DORTHEA LEIGHTON, 1944, Navaho Lives. Chapter VIII in *The Navaho Door.* Cambridge, Massachusetts.

LEVI-STRAUSS, CLAUDE, 1943, Review of *Sun Chief* by Leo W. Simmons. *Social Research,* 10: 515–517.

LINDERMAN, FRANK B., 1930, *American, the Life Story of a Great Indian.* New York: John Day Company.

———, 1932, *Red Mother.* New York: John Day Company.

LONG LANCE, CHIEF BUFFALO CHILD, 1928, *Long Lance.* New York: Cosmopolitan Book Corporation.

LOWIE, R. H., 1928, Individualforschung unter den Primitiven. In *Besonderen unter den Yamana auf Feuerland,* W. Koppers (ed.). Vienna: Schmidt-Festschrift.

———, 1935, *The Crow Indians.* New York: Holt, Rinehart and Winston.

McKENNY, THOMAS L., and JAMES HALL, 1933, *The Indian Tribes of North America, with biographical sketches and anecdoes of the principal chiefs.* A new edition, edited by Frederick Webb Hodge. 3 vols. Edinburgh, Scotland: John Grant.

McWHORTER, LUCULLUS VIRGIL, 1940, *Yellow Wolf, His Own Story.* Caldwell, Idaho: The Caxton Press.

MALINOWSKI, B., 1932, Field Method. In *Argonauts of the Western Pacific.* London: Routledge, pp. 525.

———, 1934, Whither Africa? Review of *Man of Africa* by Ntara, S. Y. *Intern. Rev. of Missions,* 25: 401–407.

MANDELBAUM, DAVID, 1941, Social Trends and Personal Pressures. In *Language, Culture and Personality,* Leslie Spier (ed.). Menasha, Wisconsin: Sapir Memorial Publication Fund.

MARQUIS, THOMAS B., 1931, *A Warrior Who Fought Custer.* Minneapolis, Minn.: The Midwest Co.

MEAD, MARGARET, 1932, *The Changing Culture of an Indian Tribe.* Columbia University Contribution to Anthropology, 15. New York: Columbia University Press.

———, 1933, More Comprehensive Field Methods. *American Anthropologist,* 35 (1): 1–15.

———, 1935, Review of *The Riddle of the Sphinx* by G. Roheim. *Character and Personality,* 4: 85–90.

———, 1940, The Mountain Arapesh. II. Supernaturalism, Field Techniques, Anthropological Papers of the American Museum of Natural History, 37, Part 3: 325–338.

———, 1944, *Cultural Approach to Personality.* Transactions of the New York Academy of Sciences, Series 2, 6: 93–101.

MICHELSON, TRUMAN, 1925, *The Autobiography of a Fox Indian Woman.* Bureau of American Ethnology Fortieth Annual Report. Washington, D.C.: Smithsonian Institution.

———, 1932, *The Narrative of a Southern Cheyenne Woman.* Smithsonian Miscellaneous Collections, 87: 13.

———, 1933, Narrative of an Arapaho Woman. *American Anthropologist,* 35: 595–610.

MOFOLO, THOMAS, 1931, *Shaka, an Historical Romance.* With an introduction by Sir Henry Newbolt. Translated from the original Sesuto by F. H. Dutton. London: Humphrey Milford.

68 · SELECTED BIBLIOGRAPHY

MORGAN, WILLIAM, 1936, *Human-wolves among the Navaho*. Yale University Publications in Anthropology, 11: 1–43.

MURRAY, WILLIAM H., 1931, *Pocahontas and Pushmataha*. Oklahoma City.

NEIHARDT, JOHN G., 1932, *Black Elk Speaks, being the life story of a holy man of the Oglala Sioux*. New York: William Morrow and Co.

NTARA, S. Y., 1934, *Man of Africa*. London: The Religious Tract Society.

OPLER, M. E., 1935, The Psychoanalytic Treatment of Culture. *Psychoanalytical Review*, 22: 138–157.

————, 1938, A Chiricahua Apache's Account of the Geronimo Campaign of 1886. *New Mexico Historical Review*, 13: 360–386.

————, 1938, Dirty Boy: A Jicarilla Tale of Raid and War. *AAA Memorial*, 52.

————, 1939, A Description of a Tonkawa Peyote Meeting Held in 1902. *American Anthropologist*, 41: 433–440.

————, 1941, *An Apache Life-way*. Chicago: University of Chicago Press.

OPLER, MARVIN K., 1942, Psychoanalytic Techniques in Social Analysis. *The Journal of Social Psychology*, 15: 91–127.

OSKISON, JOHN M., 1938, *Tecumseh and His Times. The Story of a Great Indian*. New York: Putnam.

PARSONS, ELSIE CLEWS, 1925, *A Pueblo Indian Journal 1920–1921*. Memoirs of the American Anthropological Association 32.

PASSIN, HERBERT, 1942, Tarahumara Prevarication: A Problem in Field Method. *American Anthropologist*, 44: 235–247.

PERHAM, MARGERY F., 1936, *Ten Africans*. London: Faber.

RADIN, PAUL, 1926, *Crashing Thunder, the Autobiography of an American Indian*. Paul Radin (ed.). New York: Appleton.

————, 1933, *The Method and Theory of Ethnology*. London: McGraw-Hill.

REDFIELD, ROBERT, and ALFONSO R. VILLA, 1934, *A Village Leader: A Native Autobiography*. In Chan Kom Publication No. 448 of the Carnegie Institution of Washington, pp. 212–230.

RICHARDS, A. I., 1939, The Development of Field Work Methods in Social Anthropology. In *The Study of Society*, F. C. Bartlett (ed.). New York: Macmillan.

————, 1934, *Spider Woman: A Story of Navajo Weavers and Chanters*. New York: Macmillan.

————, 1939, *Dezba: Woman of the Desert*. New York: J. J. Augustin.

SACH, WULF, 1937, *Black Hamlet, The Mind of an African Negro Revealed by Psychoanalysis*. London: Geoffrey Bles.

SANDOZ, M., 1942, *Crazy Horse: The Strange Man of the Oglalas*. New York: Knopf.

SAPIR, EDWARD, 1934, The Emergence of the Concept of Personality in a Study of Culture. *Journal of Social Psychology*, 5: 408–415.

————, 1937, The Contribution of Psychiatry to an Understanding of Behavior in Society. *American Journal of Sociology*, 42: 862–870.

————, 1938, Why Cultural Anthropology Needs the Psychiatrist. *Psychiatry*, 1: 7–12.

————, and HARRY HOIJER, 1942, *Navaho Texts*. Iowa City, Iowa: Linguistic Society of America.

————, and MORRIS SWADISH, 1939, *Nootka Texts*. Tales and Ethnological Narratives. William Dwight Whitney Linguistic Series. Philadelphia: Linguistic Society of America.

SCHACHTEL, A. H., JULES HENRY, and ZUNIA HENRY, 1942, Rorschach Analysis of Pilaga Indian Children. *The American Journal of Orthopsychiatry,* 12: 679–712.

SCHAPERA, I., 1935, Field Methods in the Study of Modern Culture Contacts. *Africa,* 8:315–328.

SELIGMAN, C. G., 1928, The Unconscious in Relation to Anthropology. *Brit. J. of Psychol.,* 18: 373–387.

————, 1929, Temperament Conflict and Psychosis in a Stone Age Population. *British Journal of Medical Psychology,* 9: 187–202.

SHAW, CLIFFORD R., 1930, *The Jack-Roller: A Delinquent Boy's Own Story.* Chicago: University of Chicago Press.

————, 1931, *The Natural History of a Delinquent Career.* Chicago: University of Chicago Press.

SIMMONS, LEO W., 1942, *Sun Chief, the autobiography of a Hopi Indian.* New Haven: Yale University Press.

SLOTKIN, J. S., 1943, Status of the Marginal Man. *Sociology and Social Research,* 28: 47–54.

SPECK, F. G., 1933, Notes on the Life of John Wilson, The Revealer of Peyote, as recalled by his nephew, George Anderson. *General Magazine & Historical Chronicle,* 36: 13–18.

SPICER, E. H., 1940, *Pascua, a Yaqui Village in Arizona.* Chicago: University of Chicago Press.

SPOTT, ROBERT, and A. L. KROEBER, 1942, *Yurok Narratives.* University of California Publications in American Archaeology and Ethnology, 35: 143–256.

STANDING BEAR, LUTHER (CHIEF), 1928, *My People the Sioux.* Boston: Houghton Mifflin.

————, 1933, *Land of the Spotted Eagle.* Boston: Houghton Mifflin.

STEWARD, JULIAN H., 1938, *Panatubiui, an Owens Valley Paiute.* Washington, D.C.: Smithsonian Institution. Bureau of American Ethnology Bulletin 119.

TAFT, JESSIE, 1933, Thirty-One Contacts with a Seven Year Old Boy. In *Dynamics of Therapy.* New York: Macmillan, pp. 113–274.

THOMPSON, LAURA, 1942, *Guam and Its People.* Studies of the Pacific No. 8. American Council, Institute of Pacific Relations.

————, and ALICE JOSEPH, 1944, *The Hopi Way.* Chicago: University of Chicago Press.

THURNWALD, HILDE, 1937, *Menschen der Sudsee.* Stuttgart: Ferdinand Enke.

THURNWALD, R., 1932, The Psychology of Acculturation. *American Anthropologist,* 34: 557–569.

TITIEV, MISCHA, 1944, Old Oraibi. Papers of the Peabody Museum of Harvard University 22, (1).

TURI, JOHAN, 1931, *Turi's Book of Lappland*. Edited and translated into Danish by Emilie Demant Hatt. (Translated from the Danish by E. Gee Nash.) London: Jonathan Cape.

UNDERHILL, RUTH, 1936, *The Autobiography of a Papago Woman*. Memoirs of the American Anthropological Association 46.

VESTAL, STANLEY, 1932, *Sitting Bull*. Boston: Houghton Mifflin.

———, 1934, *Warpath. The true story of the fighting Sioux, told in a biography of Chief White Bull*. Boston: Houghton Mifflin.

VILLA, ALFONSO R. A., 1934, Chan Kom Diary. In Chan Kom Publication No. 448 of the Carnegie Institution of Washington.

VOEGELIN, C. F., 1935, *Tubatulabal Texts*. University of California Publications in American Archaeology and Ethnology, 34: 191–246.

VOEGELIN, E., 1938, Tubatulabal Ethnography. Anthropological Records, University of California, Berkeley, 1: 72–80.

WARNER, W. LLOYD, BUFORD M. JUNKER, and WALTER A. ADAMS, 1941, Color and Human Nature. Negro personality development in a northern city. Washington D.C.: American Council on Education.

WASHBURNE, HELUIZ CHANDLER, 1940, *Land of the Good Shadows. The Life Story of Anauta, an Eskimo Woman*. New York: John Day Company.

WASSEN, HENRY, 1938, Original Documents from the Cuna Indians of San Blas, Panama. Ethnological Studies, 6. II, Biography of the High Chief, Nele De Kantule of Ustupu.

WELLS, H. G., 1935, *Experiment in Autobiography*. New York: Macmillan.

WHITE, LESLIE A., 1943, Autobiography of an Acoma Indian. In *New Material from Acoma*. Washington, D.C.: Smithsonian Institution. Bureau of American Ethnology Bulletin 136.

WHITING, JOHN, 1941, *Becoming a Kwoma*. New Haven, Conn.: Yale University Press.

WHITMAN, WILLIAM, 1939, Xube, a Ponca Autobiography. *Journal of American Folklore,* 52: 180–193.

WHORF, B. L., 1941, The Relation of Habitual Thought and Behavior to Language. In *Language, Culture and Personality,* L. Spier, A. I. Hallowell, and S. S. Newman (eds.). Menasha, Wisconsin: Sapir Memorial Publication Fund. pp. 75–93.

WILLIAMS, F. E., 1939, The Reminiscences of Ahuia Ova. *Journal of the Royal Anthropological Institute,* 49: 11–44.

WILSON, GILBERT L., n.d., *Goodbird the Indian, His Story*. New York: Fleming H. Revell Co.

———, 1928, *Hidatsa Eagle Trapping*. Anthropological Papers of the American Museum of Natural History 30, Part 4.

WYMAN, LELAND C., W. W. HILL, and IVA OSANAI, 1942, *Navajo Eschatology*. University of New Mexico Bulletin, Anthropological Series 4 (1).

ZIMMERMAN, C. L., 1941, *White Eagle: Chief of the Poncas*. Harrisburg, Pennsylvania: Telegraph Press.

1945 to Present

ABERLE, DAVID F., 1951b, *The Reconciliation of Divergent Views of Hopi Culture Through the Analysis of Life-History Material.* University Microfilms, Publication No. 2100. Ann Arbor, Michigan, copyright, 1951, by the author.

ADAIR, JOHN, 1960, A Pueblo G. I. In *In the Company of Man,* J. B. Casagrande (ed.). New York: Harper & Row, pp. 489–504.

———, n.d., Life Histories of Six Zuni Young Men. *Primary Records in Culture and Personality.* Vol. I, Bert Kaplan (ed.). Microcard Publications of Primary Records. Madison, Wisconsin: The Microcard Foundation.

ADAMS, R. N., 1951, Personnel in Culture Change: A Bit of a Hypothesis. *Social Forces,* 30: 185–189.

ALBERT, ETHEL M., 1960, My Boy Muntu. In *In the Company of Man,* J. B. Casagrande (ed.). New York: Harper & Row, pp. 357–376.

ALLPORT, G. W., J. S. BRUNER, and E. M. JANDORF, 1953, Personality Under Social Catastrophe: Ninety life-histories of the Nazi revolution. In *Personality in Nature, Society and Culture,* C. Kluckhohn and H. A. Murray (eds.). New York: Alfred A. Knopf.

ANONYMOUS, 1949–1952, Field Methods and Techniques. *Human Organization,* all issues of Vol. VIII.

AWOLOWO, OBAFEMI, 1960, *The Autobiography of Chief Obafemi Awolowo.* New York: Cambridge University Press.

BABCOCK, C. G., and W. CAUDILL, 1958, Personal and Cultural Factors in Treating a Nisei Man. In *Clinical Studies in Culture Conflict,* G. Seward (ed.). New York: Ronald Press, pp. 409–448.

BAKER, GERTRUDE, 1958, Psychodiagnosis Across the Culture Barrier. In *Clinical Studies in Culture Conflict,* G. Seward (ed.). New York: Ronald Press.

BARNETT, HOMER G., 1952, *Innovation: The Basis of Culture Change.* New York: McGraw-Hill.

———, 1957, *Indian Shakers.* Carbondale: Southern Illinois University Press.

BARNOUW, VICTOR, 1949, The Phantasy World of a Chippewa Woman. *Psychiatry: Journal for the Study of Interpersonal Relations,* 12: 67–76.

———, 1963, Life History Material. In *Culture and Personality.* Homewood, Ill.: The Dorsey Press, Chapter 7.

BAUER, RAMOND A., 1953, The Psychology of the Soviet Middle Elite: Two Case Histories. In *Personality in Nature, Society and Culture.* Kluckhohn and H. A. Murray (eds.). New York: Knopf, pp. 633–650.

———, 1955, *Nine Soviet Portraits.* New York: Technology Press of M.I.T. Wiley.

BEAGLEHOLE, ERNEST, and PEARL BEAGLEHOLE, 1946, *Some Modern Maories,* Wellington, New Zealand: Council for Educational Research.

BECKETT, J., 1958, Marginal Men: A Study of Two Half-Cast Aborigines. *Oceania,* 29: 91–108.

BENNET, J. W., 1948, The Study of Cultures: A Survey of Technique and Methodology in Field Work. *American Sociological Review,* 13: 672–689.

BIESANZ, J. M., and M. ORDONEZ, 1958, Autobiography of a Guatemalan Indian. In *Men and Cultures: Selected Papers of the Fifth International Congress of Anthropological and Ethnological Science,* A. F. C. Wallace (ed.). Philadelphia: University of Pennsylvania Press.

BOHANNAN, LAURA, 1960, The Frightened Witch. In *In the Company of Man.* J. B. Casagrande (ed.). New York: Harper & Row, pp. 377–396.

BOUGINNAN, ERIKA, n.d., A Life History of an Ojibwa Young Woman. Primary Records in Culture and Personality, Vol. 1, Bert Kaplan (ed.) Microcard Publications of Primary Records. Madison, Wisconsin: The Microcard Foundation.

BRUNER, EDWARD M., n.d., The Life History of a Fort Berthold Indian Psychotic. Primary Records in Culture and Personality. Vol. 2, Bert Kaplan (ed.). Microcard Publications of Primary Records. Madison, Wisconsin: The Microcard Foundation.

CAMPBELL, DONALD T., 1961, The Mutual Methodological Relevance of Anthropology and Psychology. In *Psychological Anthropology; Approaches to Culture and Personality,* Francis L. K. Hsu (ed.). Homewood, Ill.: The Dorsey Press.

CAROTHERS, J. C., 1948, A Study of Mental Derangement in Africans, and an attempt to Explain its Peculiarities, more Especially in Relation to the African Attitude to Life. *Psychiatry,* 11: 47–89.

CARPENTER, EDMUND, 1960, Ohnainewk, Eskimo Hunter. In *In The Company of Man,* J. B. Casagrande (ed.). New York: Harper & Row, pp. 417–426.

CARSTAIRS, G. MORRIS, 1958, *The Twice Born: A Study of a Community of High-Caste Hindus.* Bloomington: Indiana University Press.

CASAGRANDE, JOSEPH B. (ed.), 1960, John Mink, Ojibwa Informant. In *In The Company of Man,* New York: Harper & Row, pp. 467–488.

CHAMBERS, HARVEY, and ETHEL BRAUT MONTURE, 1955, *Joseph Brant: Mohawk.* East Lansing, Michigan: Michigan State.

CHAMBERS, HARVEY II, 1962, *The Last Stand of the Nez Perce: Destruction of a People.* New York: Twayne Publishers.

CHAO, B. Y., 1947, *Autobiography of a Chinese Woman.* New York:

CHAUDHURI, NIRAD C., 1951, *The Autobiography of an Unknown Indian.* New York: Macmillan.

CLEAVES, F. W., 1956, The Biography of Bayan of the Barin in the Yuan Shih. *Harvard Journal of Asiatic Studies,* 19: 3–4.

CLERC, ANDRÉ D., 1950, *Chitlangou: Son of a Chief.* United Society for Christian Literature, London: Lutterworth Press.

COLLINS, JUNE M., 1949, John Fornsby: The Personal Document of a Coast Salish Indian. In *Indians of the Urban Northwest,* Marian W. Smith (ed.). New York: Columbia University Press.

COLSON, ELIZABETH, n.d., Autobiographies of Three Pomo Women. Primary Records in Culture and Personality, Vol. 1, Bert Kaplan (ed.). Microcard Publications of Primary Records. Wisconsin: The Microcard Foundation.

CONKLIN, HAROLD C., 1960, Maling, A Hanunóo Girl from the Philippines: A Day in Pariwa. In *In the Company of Man*, J. B. Casagrande (ed.). New York: Harper & Row, pp. 101–119.

CRUTWELL, N. E. G., 1959, *Peter Posaro: A Papuan's Progress.* Sydney, Australia: Board of Missions.

CUNNISON, IAN, 1960, The Onda. In *In the Company of Man*, J. B. Casagrande (ed.). New York: Harper & Row, pp. 309–332.

DAI, BRIGHAM, 1957, Obsessive-Compulsive Disorders in Chinese Culture. *Social Problems,* 4: 313–321; also in *Culture and Mental Health,* M. K. Opler (ed.). New York: Macmillan.

D'ANDRADE, ROY G., 1961, Anthropological Studies of Dreams. In *Psychological Anthropology: Approach to Culture and Personality.* Francis L. K. Hsu (ed.). Homewood, Ill.: The Dorsey Press.

DELF, G., 1962, *Jomo Kenyatta.* New York: Doubleday.

DEVEREUX, GEORGE, 1945, The Logical Foundations of Culture and Personality Studies. *Trans. N. Y. Acad. Sciences,* 2: 7.

———, 1951, *Reality and Dream: Psychotherapy of a Plains Indian.* New York: International University Press.

———, 1957, Psychoanalysis as Anthropological Field Work: Data and Theoretical Implications. *Trans. N.Y. Acad. Sciences, Series 2,* 19: 457–472.

DOLLARD, JOHN, 1953, The Life History in Community Studies. In *Personality in Nature, Society and Culture,* Clyde Kluckhohn, and Henry A. Murray (eds.). New York: Alfred A. Knopt.

DUBOIS, CORA, 1960, The Form and Substance of Status: A Javanese-American Relationship. In *In the Company of Man*, J. B. Casagrande (ed.). New York: Harper & Row, pp. 211–232.

DYK, WALTER, 1947, *A Navaho Autobiography.* Viking Fund Publication in Anthropology, No. 8.

EGGAN, DOROTHY, n.d., Hopi Dreams and a Life History Sketch. Primary Records in Culture and Personality, Vol. 2, Bert Kaplan (ed.). Microcard Publications of Primary Records. Madison, Wisconsin: The Microcard Foundation.

———, 1949, The Significance of Dreams for Anthropological Research. *American Anthropologist,* 51.

———, 1952, The Manifest Content of Dreams: A Challenge to Social Science. *American Anthropologist,* 54.

———, 1961, Dream Analysis, In *Studying Personality Cross-Culturally,* Bert Kaplan. New York: Harper & Row.

ENGELMANN, H. O., 1960, The Activity Bias of Ethnography and the History of Society. *Anthropological Quarterly,* 33: 158–163.

ENGLISH, O. SPURGEON, and STUART M. FINCH, 1954, *Introduction to Psychiatry.* New York: Norton (See Chapter 4, History Taking, Examination, and Diagnosis, pp. 70–100.)

ERASMUS, C. J., 1952, The Leader Vs. Tradition: A Case Study. *American Anthropologist,* 54: 168–178.

ERIKSON, ERIK H., 1958, *Young Man Luther.* New York: Norton.

FALKNER, D., 1946, Witch or What? *Nigeria,* 23: 105–111. Lagos.

FANTL, BERTA, 1959, Cultural Factors in Family Diagnosis of a Chinese Family. *International Journal of Social Psychiatry,* 5: 27–32.

FIELD, MARGARET J., 1948, *Akim-Kotoku: An Oman of the Gold Coast.* London: Crown Agents for the Colonies.

———, 1955, Witchcraft as a Primitive Interpretation of Mental Disorder. *Journal of Mental Science,* 101: 826–833.

FIRTH, RAYMOND, 1953, The Study of Values by Social Anthropologists. *Man,* 53: 232.

———, 1960, A Polynesian Aristocrat. In *In the Company of Man,* J. B. Casagrande (ed.). New York: Harper & Row, pp. 1–40.

FORSBROOK, H. A., 1955, The Life of Justin. Part I. An African autobiography translated and anotated. *Tanganyika Notes Record,* 41: 31–57.

———, 1956, The Life of Justin. Part 2. An African autobiography. *Tanganyika Notes Record,* 42: 19–30.

FROMM, ERICH, 1949, Psychoanalytic Characterology and Its Application to the Understanding of Culture. In *Culture and Personality,* Sargent and Smith (eds.). New York: The Viking Fund.

GARDNER, R., 1960, A Human Document. *Daedalus,* 89.

GARRATY, JOHN, 1957, *The Nature of Biography.* New York: Knopf.

GARST, SHANNON, 1953, *Chief Joseph of the Nez Perce.* New York: Messmer.

GILLIN, JOHN, 1948, Magical Fright. *Psychiatry,* 11: 387–400.

GLADWIN, THOMAS, 1960, Petrus Mailo, Chief of Moen. In *In the Company of Man,* J. B. Casagrande (ed.). New York: Harper & Row, pp. 41–62.

——— and SEYMOUR B. SARASON, 1953, *Truk: Man in Paradise.* New York: Viking Fund Publications in Anthropology No. 20.

———, 1959, Culture and Individual Personality Integration on Truk. In *Culture and Mental Health,* Marvin Opler (ed.). New York: Macmillan.

GLASSE, ROBERT M., 1959, Revenge and Redress Among the Huli: A Preliminary Account. *Mankind,* 5: 273–288.

HALLOWELL, A. I., 1938, Shabwan: A Dissocial Indian Girl. *The American Journal of Orthopsychiatry,* 8: 329–340.

———, 1945, Sociopsychological Aspects of Acculturation. In *The Science of Man in the World Crisis,* Ralph Linton (ed.). New York: Columbia University Press.

———, 1951, The Projective Technique in the Sociopsychological Study of Acculturation. *Journal of Projective Techniques,* 15: 27.

———, 1953, Culture, Personality, and Society. In *Anthropology Today,* A. L. Kroeber (ed.). Chicago: University of Chicago Press.

———, 1954, Psychological Leads for Ethnological Field Workers. In *Personal Character and Cultural Milieu,* Haring (ed.). New York: Syracuse University Press. 1956.

———, 1955, *Culture and Experience.* Philadelphia: University of Pennsylvania Press.

HANDLEY, K. N., 1957, *Four Case Studies in Hawaii: Intercultural Problems and the Practice of Social Work.* Honolulu: University of Hawaii Press.

HANKS, L. M., JR., 1949, The Locus of Individual Differences in Certain Primitive Cultures. In *Culture and Personality*. New York: The Viking Fund, Inc.

————, and HERBERT PHILLIPS, 1961, A Young Thai From the Countryside. In *Studying Personality Cross-Culturally*, Bert Kaplan (ed.). New York: Harper & Row.

HART, C. W. M., 1954, The Sons of Turimpi. *American Anthropologist*, 56: 242–261.

HAUCK, P. A., 1955, Ute Rorschach Performances and Some Notes on Field Problems and Methods. Salt Lake City: University of Utah Anthropological Papers 23.

HENRY, JULES, 1949, Cultural Objectification of the Case History. *American Journal of Orthopsychiatry*, 19: 655–673.

HENRY, WILLIAM E., 1947, The Thematic Apperception Technique in the Study of Culture-Personality Relations. *Genet. Psychol. Monographs*, 35.

————, 1951, The Thematic Apperception Technique in the Study of Group and Cultural Problems. In *An Introduction to Projective Techniques and other Devices for Understanding the Dynamics of Human Behavior*, Harold H. and Gladys L. Anderson (eds.). New York: Prentice-Hall.

HERSKOVITS, MELVILLE J., 1948, *Man and His Works*. The Ethnographer's Laboratory. New York: Knopf, pp. 79–93.

————, 1950, The Hypothetical Situation: A Technique of Field Research. *Southwestern Journal of Anthropology*, VI: 32–40.

HITCHCOCK, JOHN T., 1960, Surat Singh, Head Judge. In *In the Company of Man*, J. B. Casagrande (ed.). New York: Harper & Row, pp. 233–272.

HONIGMANN, JOHN J. The Life History of a Pathon (Pakistan) Young Man. Primary Records in Culture and Personality, Vol. 1, Bert Kaplan (ed.). Microcard Publications of Primary Records. Madison, Wisconsin: The Microcard Foundation.

————, 1949, *Culture and Ethos of Kaska Society*. Yale University Publications in Anthropology No. 40. New Haven, Conn.

————, 1961, The Interpretation of Dreams in Anthropological Field Work: A Case Study. In *Studying Personality Cross-Culturally*, Bert Kaplan (ed.). New York: Harper & Row.

HOOK, SIDNEY, n.d., *The Hero in History*. Boston: Beacon Press.

HOROWITZ, M., 1956, Psychological Needs As a Function of Social Environments. In *The State of the Social Sciences*, L. D. White (ed.). Chicago: University of Chicago Press.

HSU, FRANCIS L. K., 1952, Anthropology or Psychiatry: A Definition of Objectives and Their Implications. *Southwestern Journal of Anthropology*, 8: 1952.

————, 1961, *Psychological Anthropology: Approaches to Culture and Personality*. Homewood, Ill.: Dorsey Press.

HUDDLE, J. G., 1957, The Life of Yakobo Adoko of Lango District. *Uganda Journal*, 21: 184–190.

JAMES, BERNARD J., 1954, Some Critical Observations Concerning Analysis of

Chippewa "Atomism" and Chippewa Personality. *American Anthropology,* 56: 283–886.

JARAMILLO, C. M., 1955. *Romance of a Little Village Girl.* San Antonio: Naylor Co.

JEWELL, DONALD P., 1952, A Case of A "Psychotic" Navaho Indian Male. *Human Organization,* 11:32–36.

JOSEPH, ALICE, and V. F. MURRAY, 1951, *Chamorros and Coaclinins of Saipan.* Cambridge: Harvard University Press.

KAPLAN, BERT, 1957, Personality and Social Structure. In *Review of Sociology,* Gittler (ed.). New York: Wiley.

———, 1961, *Studying Personality Cross-Culturally.* New York: Harper & Row.

KARDINER, ABRAM, 1945, The Concept of Basic Personality Structure As an Operational Tool in the Social Sciences. In *The Science of Man in the World Crisis,* R. Linton (ed.). New York: Columbia University Press.

———, 1958, Psychoanalysis and Anthropology. In *Science and Psychoanalysis,* J. H. Masserman (ed.). New York: Grune & Stratton.

———, and LIONEL OVESY, 1951, *The Mark of Oppression.* New York: Meridian.

KARVE, D. D. (ed.), 1963, *The New Bramans, Five Maharashtrian Families.* Berkeley, Calif.: University of California Press.

KAZEM, MOHAMED 1, n.d., Autobiographies of Five Egyptian Young Women. Primary Records in Culture and Personality, Vol. 2, Bert Kaplan (ed.). *Microcard Publications of Primary Records.* Madison, Wisconsin: The Microcard Foundation.

KLINEBERG, OTTO, 1949, Recent Studies of National Character. In *Culture and Personality,* Sargent and Smith (eds.). New York: The Viking Fund.

KLUCKHOHN, CLYDE, 1946, Personality Formation Among the Navaho Indians. *Sociometry,* 9: 128–132.

———, 1949, Needed Refinements in the Biographical Approach. In *Culture and Personality,* Sargent and Smith (eds.). New York: The Viking Fund.

———, and D. LEIGHTON, 1947, *The Navaho,* Cambridge, Massachusetts: Harvard University Press.

———, and J. ROSENZWEIG, 1947, Two Navaho Children over a Five-Year Period. *American Journal of Orthopsychiatry,* 19: 266–278.

———, 1956a, The Influence of Psychiatry on Anthropology During the Past One Hundred Years. In *Personal Character and Cultural Milieu,* Douglas G. Haring (ed.). New York: Syracuse University Press.

———, 1956b, A Navaho Personal Document with a Brief Paretian Analysis. In *Personal Character and Culture Milieu,* Douglas G. Haring (ed.). New York: Syracuse University Press.

———, 1960, A Navaho Politician. In *In the Company of Man,* J. B. Casagrande (ed.). New York: Harper & Row, pp. 439–466.

———, and W. MORGAN, 1951, Some notes on Navaho Dreams. In *Psychoanalysis and Culture,* G. B. Wilbur and W. Meunsterberger (eds.). New York: International Universities Press.

————, and H. A. MURRAY (eds.), 1953, *Personality in Nature, Society and Culture*. New York: Knopf.

KROEBER, A. L., 1945, The Use of Autobiographical Evidence. In A Yurok War Reminiscence. *Southwestern Journal of Anthropology,* 1: 318–322.

————, 1947, A Southwestern Personality Type. *Southwestern Journal of Anthropology,* 3: 108–113.

KROEBER, THEODORE, 1961, *Ishi in Two Worlds: A Biography of the Last Wild Indian in North America.* Berkeley: University of California Press.

LaBARRE, WESTON, n.d., The Autobiography of a Kiowa Indian. Primary Records in Culture and Personality, Vol. 2, Bert Kaplan (ed.). *Microcard Publications of Primary Records.* Madison, Wisconsin: The Microcard Foundation.

LAMBO, T. A., 1955, The Role of Cultural Factors in Paranoid Psychosis Among the Yoruba Tribe. *Journal of Mental Science,* 101: 239–266.

LANDES, RUTH, 1938, The Abnormal Among the Ojibwa Indians. *Journal of Abnormal and Social Psychology,* 33: 14–33.

LANTIS, MARGARET, 1960, *Eskimo Childhood and Interpersonal Relationships: Nunivak Biographies and Genealogies.* Seattle: University of Washington Press.

LAURENTIN, ANNE, 1963, Nzakara Women. In *Women of Tropical Africa,* Denise Paulme (ed.). Berkeley and Los Angeles: University of California Press.

LAYE, CARMARA, 1954, *The Dark Child.* New York: Noonday Press.

LEIGHTON, ALEXANDER H., and DOROTHEA LEIGHTON, 1949, Gregorio, the Hand Trembler: A Psychobiological Personality of a Navaho Indian. Papers of the Peabody Museum of American Archaeology and Ethnology, 40 (1).

LEIGHTON, DOROTHEA, and CLYDE KLUCKHOHN, 1947, *Children of the People: The Navaho Individual and His Development.* Cambridge, Mass.: Harvard University Press.

LESLIE, C. M., 1960, *Now We Are Civilized: A Study of the World View of the Zapotec Indians of Mitla, Oaxaca.* Detroit: Wayne State University Press.

LESSA, W. A., and M. SPIEGELMAN, 1954, *Ulithian Personality as Seen Through Ethnological Materials and Thematic Test Analysis.* University of California Publications in Culture and Society 2.

LEWIS, OSCAR, 1959, *Five Familes: Mexican Case Studies in the Culture of Poverty.* New York: Basic Books.

————, 1964, *Pedro Martinez.* New York: Random House.

LIN, TSUNG-YI, 1953, A Study of the Incidence of Mental Disorder in Chinese and Other Cultures. *Psychiatry,* 16: 313–336.

LINTON, RALPH, 1945, *The Cultural Background of Personality.* New York: Appleton.

————, 1956, *Culture and Mental Disorders,* G. Devereaux (ed.). Springfield, Ill.: Charles C Thomas.

LITTLE, K. L., 1948, The Changing Position of Women in the Sierra Leone Protectorate. *Africa,* 18: 1–17.

LOBSANG, R. T., 1956, *The Third Eye: The Autobiography of a Tibetan Lama.* London: Secke & Warburg.

LOCKWOOD, DOUGLAS, 1962, *I, the Aboriginal.* Australia: Rigby Limited.

LOWIE, ROBERT H., 1960, My Crow Interpreter. In *In the Company of Man,* J. B. Casagrande (ed.). New York: Harper & Row, pp. 427–438.

LUCIER, C., 1958, Prenatal Memories of an Eskimo Man. Anthropological Papers of the University of Alaska, 6 (2): 122.

LURIE, NANCY O., 1961, *Mountain Wolf Woman, Sister of Crashing Thunder: The Autobiography of a Winnebago Woman.* Ann Arbor, Mich.: University of Michigan Press.

LUTHULI, ALBERT, 1962, *Let My People Go: An Autobiography.* Johnnesburg: Collins.

MACGREGOR, GORDEN, 1946, *Warriors without Weapons.* Chicago: University of Chicago Press.

MACOBY, E. E., and NATHAN MACOBY, 1954, The Interview: A Tool of Social Science. In *The Handbook of Social Psychology,* Gardner Lindzey, (ed.). Reading, Mass.: Addison-Wesley, pp. 449–487.

MAHER, R. F., 1961, *New Men of Papua: A Study in Culture Change.* Madison: University of Wisconsin Press.

MANDELBAUM, DAVID G., 1960, A Reformer of His People. In *In the Company of Man,* J. B. Casagrande (ed.). New York: Harper & Row, pp. 273–308.

MARRIOTT, ALICE, 1948, *Maria: The Potter of San Ildefonso.* Norman: University of Oklahoma Press.

MEAD, MARGARET, 1949, The Mountain Arapesh, V., The Record of Unabelin with Rorschach Analyses. Anthropological Papers of the American Museum of Natural History No. 40.

———, 1952a, Anthropological Models for the Study of Culture at a Distance (the Single Informant; the Study of Living Communities). In Research in Contemporary Cultures: A Manual on Theory and Practice in the Study of Culture at a Distance by Inter-disciplinary Groups, Margaret Mead and Rhoda Metraux. Manuscript.

———, 1952b, Some Relationships Between Social Anthropology and Psychiatry. In *Dynamic Psychiatry.* F. Alexander and H. Ross (eds.). Chicago: University of Chicago Press.

———, 1960, Weaver of the Border. In *In the Company of Man,* J. B. Casagrande (ed.). New York: Harper & Row, pp. 175–210.

MENSH, IVAN N. and JULES HENRY, 1953, Direct Observations and Psychological Tests in Anthropological Field Work. *American Anthropologist,* 55.

METRAUX, A., 1942, A Quechua Messiah In Eastern Penu. *American Anthropologist,* 44: 721–725.

MOLINA, M. F., 1947, Study of a Psychopathic Personality in Guatemala. *Psychiatry,* 10: 31–36.

MOORE, G., 1957, Amos Tutuloa, A. Nigerian Visionary. *Black Orpheus,* 1: 27–35.

MPHAHLELE, E. L., 1959, *Down Second Avenue.* London: Faber.

MURRAY, HENRY A., 1955, *Introduction to Clinical Studies of Personality*, Arthur Burton and Robert E. Harris (eds.). New York: Harper & Row, pp. 1–17.

NADEL, S. F., 1951, *The Foundations of Social Anthropology*. New York: Free Press, pp. 35–74.

NEWMAN, PHILIP L., 1964, "Wild Man" Behavior in a New Guinea Highlands Community. *American Anthropologist*, 66: 1–19.

OAKES, MAUD, 1951, *The Two Crosses of Todos Santos: Survivals of Mayan Religious Ritual*. New York: Bollingen Foundation, Inc.

OLINGER, L. B., and V. S. SOMMERS, 1958, The Divided Path: Psychocultural Neurosis in Nisei Man. In *Clinical Studies in Culture Conflict*, G. Seward (ed.). New York: Ronald, pp. 359–408.

OPLER, MARVIN K., 1959, Dream Analysis in Ute Indian Therapy. In *Culture and Mental Health*, Marvin K. Opler (ed.). New York: Macmillan.

———, 1948, Theories of Culture and the Deviant. Proceedings of the Spring Conference of Education and the Exceptional Child. Langhorne, Pennsylvania: Child Research Clinic, The Woods Schools, pp. 8–14.

PAULME, DENISE (ed.)., 1963, *Women of Tropical Africa*. Berkeley and Los Angeles: University of California Press.

PERHAM, MARGERY (ed.). *Ten Africans*. Evanston, Ill.: Northwestern University Press.

POINANT, A. H. E., 1957, *Piccaninny Walkabout: A Story of Two Aboriginal Children*. Sidney: Angus & Robertson.

POZAS, RICARDO, 1962, *Juan the Chamula: An Ethnological Re-Creation of the Life of a Mexican Indian*. Berkeley: University of California Press.

PRUITT, IDA, 1945, *A Daughter of the Han: The Autobiography of a Chinese Working Woman*. New Haven, Conn.: Yale University Press.

ROBERTS, G. H., and G. E. HYCLE, 1959, Ancestry of Latakuts Kalahar (Fancy Eagle). *Nebraska History*, 40: 67–73.

ROBERTS, JOHN M., 1951, Three Navaho Households: A Comparative Study of Small Group Culture. Papers of the Peabody Museum of American Archeology and Ethnology, 40, No. 3, Harvard University.

———, 1959, *Four Southwestern Men: A Study in Culture, Culture Control and Values*. Lincoln: University of Nebraska Press.

ROHEIM, GEZA, 1947, Dream Analysis and Field Work in Anthropology. In *Psychoanalysis and the Social Sciences 1*, Geza Roheim (ed.). New York:

———, 1950, *Psychoanalysis and Anthropology: Culture, Personality, and the Unconscious*. New York.

ROHER, JOHN H., and MUNRO S. EDMONSON, 1960, *The Eighth Generation: Cultures and Personalities of New Orleans Negroes*. New York: Harper & Row.

SACHES, WULF, 1947, *Black Anger*. Enlarged edition of Black Hamlet. Boston: Little, Brown.

SASLOW, G., and E. D. CHAPPLE, 1945, A New Life-History Form with Instructions for Its Use. *Applied Anthropology*, 4: 1–18.

SCHWARTZ, THEODORE, 1962, The Palian Movement in the Admiralty Islands,

1946–54. New York Anthropological Papers of the American Museum of Natural History, 49(2): 207–422.

SEABURY, R. I., 1945, *Daughter of Africa.* Boston: Pilgrim Press.

SEWARD, G. (ed.), 1958, *Clinical Studies in Culture Conflict.* New York: Ronald Press.

SLOTKIN, J. S., 1959, Case Study and Autobiography of a Menomine Indian Paranoid Schizophrenic Man with Rorschach Analysis by George D. Spindler. Primary Records in Culture and Personality, Vol. 2, Bert Kaplan (ed.). *Microcard Publications of Primary Records.* Madison, Wisconsin: The Microcard Foundation.

SMITH, E. W., 1957, *Great Lion of Bechuanaland: The Life and Times of Roger Price, Missionary.* London: Independent Press.

SMITH, M. F., 1954, *Baba of Karo.* London: Faber.

SMITH, M. G., 1959, Dark Puritan, the Life and Work of Norman Paul. *Carribean Quarterly* 5: 34–47.

———, 1959, Dark Puritan: Part 3, Work and Woman Trouble. *Carribean Quarterly,* 6.

SPICER, JOSEPH, and CHESKY SPICER, 1949, *The Desert People: A Study of the Papago Indians.* Chicago: University of Chicago Press.

SPINDLER, GEORGE D., 1955, Sociocultural and Psychological Processes in Menomini Acculturation. University of California Publications in Culture and Society Vol. 5.

———, 1952, Personality and Peyotism in Menomini Indian Acculturation, *Psychiatry.* 15: 151–159.

———, n.d., Autobiographic Interviews of Eight Menomini Indian Males. Primary Records in Culture and Personality, Vol. 2, Bert Kaplan (ed.). *Microcard Publications of Primary Records.* Madison, Wisconsin: The Microcard Foundations.

———, and LOUISE S. SPINDLER, 1957, *American Indian Personality Types and Their Sociocultural Roots.* Annals of the American Academy of Political and Social Science 311.

SPINDLER, LOUISE S., n.d., Sixty-one Rorschachs and Fifteen Expressive Autobiographic Interviews of Menomini Indian Women. Primary Records in Culture and Personality, Vol. 2, Bert Kaplan (ed.). *Microcard Publications of Primary Records.* Madison, Wisconsin: The Microcard Foundation.

———, and GEORGE SPINDLER, 1961, A Modal Personality Technique in the Study of Menomini Acculturation. In *Studying Personality Cross-Culturally,* Bert Kaplan (ed.). New York: Harper & Row.

———, 1962, *Menomini Women and Culture Change.* Memoirs of the American Anthropological Association 91.

SPIRO, MELFORD E., 1950, A Psychotic Personality in the South Seas. *Psychiatry,* 13.

———, 1959, Cultural Heritage, Personal Tensions, and Mental Illness in a South Sea Culture. In *Culture and Mental Health,* Marvin K. Opler (ed.). New York: Macmillan, pp. 141–171.

STANNER, W. E. H., 1960, Durmugam, A Nangiomeri. In *In the Company of Man,* J. B. Casagrande (ed.). New York: Harper & Row, pp. 63–100.

STURTEVANT, WILLIAM C., 1960, A Seminole Medicine Maker. In *In the Company of Man,* J. B. Casagrande (ed.). New York: Harper & Row, pp. 505–532.

TEICHER, MORTON, 1954, Three Cases of Psychosis Among the Eskimos. *Journal of Mental Science,* 100: 527–535.

THOMAS, J. E., 1961, Kanyata and His Times. *Northern Rhodesia Journal,* 4.

THOMPSON, LAURA, 1950, *Culture in Crisis: A Study of the Hopi Indians.* New York: Harper & Row.

TILAK, LAKSHORIBA, 1950, *I Follow After: An Autobiography.* London: Oxford University Press.

TIRABUTANA, P., 1958, *A Simple One: The Story of a Siamese Girlhood.* Ithaca, N.Y.: Cornell University Press.

TOZZER, ALFRED M., 1953, *Biography and Biology. In Personality in Nature, Society, and Cultures,* C. Kluckhohn, H. A. Murray (eds.). New York: Knopf, pp. 226–242.

TUCKER, GLENN, 1956, *Tecumseh: Vision of Glory.* New York: Bobbs-Merrill.

TURNBULL, COLIN M., 1962, *The Lonely African.* New York: Simon and Schuster.

TURNER, VICTOR W., 1960, Muchona the Hornet, Interpreter of Religion. In *In the Company of Man,* J. B. Casagrande (ed.). New York: Harper & Row., pp. 333–356.

VANSTONE, J. W. (ed.), 1957, The Autobiography of an Alaskan Eskimo. *Arctic,* 10: 195–210.

VOGET, F., 1948, Individual Motivations in the Diffusion of the Wind River Shoshone Sun Dance to the Crow Indians. *American Anthropologist,* 50: 634–646.

———, 1950, A Shoshone Innovation. *American Anthropologist,* 52: 53–63.

VOGT, EVON Z., JR., n.d., Life Histories of Fourteen Navaho Young Men. Primary Records in Culture and Personality, Vol. 1, Bert Kaplan (ed.). *Microcard Publications of Primary Records.* Madison, Wisconsin: The Microcard Foundation.

WAGLEY, CHARLES, 1960, Champukwi of the Village of the Tapias. In *In the Company of Man,* J. B. Casagrande (ed.). New York: Harper & Row, pp. 397–416.

WALDRAUEN-JOHNSON, 1957, *The White Comanche: The Story of Cynthia Ann Parker and Her Son Quanah.* New York: Coment Press Books.

WALLACE, ANTHONY F. C., 1949, *King of the Delawares: Teedyuscung 1700-1763.* Philadelphia: University of Pennsylvania Press.

WALLACE, ANTHONY F. C., Individual Differences and Cultural Uniformities. *American Sociological Review,* 17.

———, 1952, Some Psychological Determinants of Culture Change in an Iroquoian Community. In *Symposium on Local Diversity in Iroquois Culture,* W. N. Fenton (ed.). Washington: B. A. E. Bulletin 150.

———, 1956, Stress and Rapid Personality Changes. *International Record of Medicine,* 169.

———, 1958, Dreams and the Wishes of the Soul. *American Anthropologist,* 60.

WARNER, W. L, 1958, *A Black Civilization: A Social Study of an Australian Tribe.* New York: Harper & Row.

WATSON, JAMES B., 1960, A New Guinea "Opening Man." In *In the Company of Man,* J. B. Casagrande (ed.). New York: Harper & Row, pp. 127–174.

WHITING, JOHN W. M., 1959, Sorcery, Sin and the Superego: A Cross-Cultural Study of Some Mechanisms of Social Control. In *Nebraska Symposium on Motivation,* M. R. Jones, (ed.). Lincoln, Nebraska.

————, 1961, Socialization Process and Personality. In *Psychological Anthropology: Approaches to Culture and Personality,* Francis L. K. Hsu (ed.). Homewood, Ill.: The Dorsey Press.

WHYTE, W. F., 1951, Observational Field Work Methods. In *Research Methods in Social Relations,* M. Jahoda, M. Deutsch, and S. W. Cook (eds.). New York: Dryden Press, pp 493–514

WILLIAMS, HERBERT H., n.d., Sixteen Autobiographical Dream Series of Moslem Maronite Men and Women. Primary Records in Culture and Personality, Vol. 4, Bert Kaplan (ed.). *Microcard Publications of Primary Records.* Madison, Wisconsin: The Microcard Foundation.

WINTER, EDWARD H., 1959, *Beyond the Mountains of the Moon: The Lives of Four Africans. Uganda.* Urbana: University of Illinois Press.

YOGANANA, PARAMHANSA, 1947, *Autobiography of a Yogi.* Los Angeles: Self-Realization Fellowship.

DATE DUE